MW00935413

13
43

A Spiritual Belief, A Way of Life, And Much More

REINCARNATION...

STEPPING STONES

OF LIFE

M. DON SCHORN

Library of Congress Cataloging-in-Publication Data
Schorn, M. Don – 1947 -
"Reincarnation...Stepping Stones of Life" by M. Don Schorn
The theory of reincarnation viewed from extensive research
1. Reincarnation 2. Ancient Texts 3. Life Mysteries
I.   Schorn, M. Don 1947 -   II. Title

Library of Congress Catalog Number: 2009924867
ISBN-13: 978-1517634513
ISBN-10: 1517634512

Cover Layout by www.enki3d.com

Book set in Times New Roman font

Other Books by M. Don Schorn:

First Journal of the Ancient Ones

Elder Gods of Antiquity

Second Journal of the Ancient Ones

Legacy of the Elder Gods

Third Journal of the Ancient Ones

Gardens of the Elder Gods

Fourth Journal of the Ancient Ones

History of the Elder Gods

A Novel of Modern Exploration, Discovery, & Ancient
Revelations, Set in the Near Future

Emerging Dawn

TABLE OF CONTENTS

Introduction

In our quest to understand life's purpose and meaning, we seek answers in a variety of ways and places. The abstract nature of this search, along with the mysterious essence of our life force, does not readily produce tangible answers within such a metaphysical pursuit. Of various paths taken in search of meaningful discovery, the belief in reincarnation has provided me with tangible understanding and real comfort, while also offering substantial answers and finite direction. Solace and enlightenment may be derived from this belief, if an open mind is maintained.

Unfortunately, much misunderstanding and skepticism surrounds this subject, labeling such a belief as absurd, ludicrous, foolish, and irreverent; to name just a few of the lesser objections. Revelations derived during times of personal introspection, often during periods of traumatic disruption, have exposed certain tenets that seemingly fit together like pieces of a puzzle.

Having been raised strict Catholic since birth, I was quickly made aware of the Church's afterlife position on heaven, hell, and purgatory at an early age. Yet I recall at age five and six that I innately knew our immortality involved the process of reincarnation, perhaps as a retained intuitive instinct, which directly contradicted my Catholic teachings. I juggled these conflicting beliefs well into adulthood until I finally undertook an effort to reconcile my spiritual beliefs with something that made sense.

Realizations from that search exposed certain precepts that appear to be key elements in providing answers to the mysteries surrounding the meaning of life. For me, the concept of reincarnation helped to explain aspects associated with the grand purpose of mortal existence, while also revealing what may happen beyond physical death. Further, it establishes a practical philosophy or way-of-life, one that consistently provides help and guidance that may assist each of us throughout every day existence. It offers logical explanations for the seeming inequities, injustices, and inexplicable nature of physical life; while also providing ultimate fairness when viewed from an all-encompassing perspective of a larger picture. If one chooses to reject a belief in continuing cycles of incarnation, perhaps the resultant life-philosophy contained within this writing might still provide some comfort and direction.

This book is not presented as proof for this concept, or to invalidate other conflicting but more conventional doctrines. Nor does it offer case studies of unexplained manifestations that occasionally occur, which seem to confound all known physical laws of nature and human understanding. Rather, the intent of this book is to define and explain, in earthly descriptive terms, merely the basics of the reincarnation process. From that enlightened perspective, each reader may conclude its validity and merit, or simply ignore its value by exercising free will choice. An open mind and a desire to evaluate spiritual alternatives will allow an objective exploration of this concept, while also revealing its simplicity of design and ultimate fairness.

PART ONE

COMPREHENSION

&

TERMINOLOGY

Chapter One

Searching

"Imagine there's no heaven." That may not be as easy as the John Lennon song suggests. "No hell below us"? Such idle speculation is also hard to accept. To where would we wish away our worst enemies? We have been indoctrinated with the concept of a religious heaven and hell since our earliest memories. Society bombards us with constant reminders. Many cultural identities, actions, foods, unique customs, languages, as well as most holidays are all rooted deep within a religious belief system that contains a reward or punishment mentality. Such ideology may be used as a tool to modify our behavior, direct our lives, or control our actions through its use as a threat or a recompense; usually with the intent of coercing individual conformity within some arbitrary 'acceptable' range of 'normal behavior.' Such conformity is often merely a form of dominance exerted by organized religions over its followers, generally through the use of fear, as well as an accompanying greed motive.

Religions attempting to transcend such a punishment mentality seem to fall short, even when focusing on the 'love of God' rather than some foreboding aspect of impending fear (often in an attempt to stop decreasing membership), since an apocalyptic 'wrath of God' deterrent remains ever present as an underlying belief. Further, the promise of an eternal reward in heaven is meant to appeal to our human weakness and inclination toward greed.

Must humankind always be prodded to perform in a certain manner, solely predicated on the promise of a reward for performing some desired action? Or can humanity

3

overcome its inherent greed and punishment mentality to transcend to a higher plane, thereby leading an exemplary life of 'righteous action,' merely for its own merit? Such a transition would allow one to live life by directing their corresponding daily actions and responses in a manner that is compassionate, moral, just, righteous, and caring; solely because it makes the most sense, and instinctively appears to be the correct and proper way in which to act. Such a life style would seemingly offer an efficient and harmonious approach to living mortal life, allowing peaceful, productive, and positive cohabitation and interaction with all others on Earth. Leading such a life style would seemingly result in meaningful consequences and ensuing progress for anyone following that pursuit. While such a noble approach is certainly idealistic, it might be an unobtainable and unrealistic expectation, if it is totally devoid of some sort of reward as an added enticement.

It can be argued whether humanity would freely choose to behave in such an exemplary manner without some type of incentive. The true meaning of any belief, and hence its real value, is found in the sum of its practical applications. One of the principle beliefs held by the Chinese philosopher Confucius (551-479 BC) professed that humankind should strive for virtue, based solely on its own merit, not because of any potential reward either during present life or within some afterlife. Such a belief is altruistic, and perhaps merely a simplistic approach to life. But it is also a noble and positive one, with ensuing enlightenment as its own underlying reward.

The majority of organized religions around the world seem to be based on a 'ledger and balance' concept. Such a belief asserts that the salvation of our immortal essence can be achieved by transcending our deceased body, thereby obtaining Heaven, Nirvana, Elysium, Valhalla, or whatever one might call their personal concept of an ethereal utopia. Where is the definitive and tangible proof that such a place exists? Not one of us has any conclusive first-hand experience, or knows another person who has irrefutably completed such a journey to the 'other-side,' regardless if such a visit was to heaven or hell. Yet we continue to believe on 'blind faith' that a better world awaits us, because we need to hold onto the concept that life does have some underlying meaning and purpose. That belief prompts humankind to strive for Good rather than Evil, through an assurance that some greater underlying Master Plan exists, one associated with a highly desirable eternal existence.

Yet it is possible that physical life has no grand or meaningful underlying purpose, beyond its obvious potential for experiencing 'everyday' mortal life. Perhaps corporeal life is as random and directionless as sparks emitted from a grinding wheel. Perhaps there is no Higher Power observing the developing 'whole' of life. Little comfort can be found within Earth's historic record, when based on longevity-of-rule associated with physical life. The longest reigning and most successful group or species of life ever to inhabit Earth were the 'terrible lizards' we call dinosaurs, creatures that are now extinct. The purpose and meaning for their very existence must now be brought into question, except for their obvious value as decayed fossil-fuel, as well as topical content for present day books, motion pictures, and their skeletal display in museums.

But if life were intrinsically linked with some underlying purpose, then it would seem natural that such a purpose would be a logical one, one that made sense while also providing universal fairness. So humanity continues to seek truth within the many varied spiritual belief systems currently available. As we pursue answers to life's mysteries, all too often only additional questions are found. But perhaps physical life only produces questions. We tend to look outward for enlightenment and direction, but perhaps those answers simply lay completely within ourselves.

Humankind's morbid curiosity with an unseen afterlife

5

continues to fuel this search through evaluation of all the known or discernible distinctions between life and death within our limited framework of understanding. Hence, the meaning of mortal life and its inevitable demise continues to harbor intrigue, as do the elusive answers to its many enigmatic unknowns. Since no real proof has ever been presented as to what actually transpires upon cessation of physical life, the essence of an afterlife belief must continue to remain purely speculative.

It is interesting to note that the most diverse religious teachings and precepts often arrive at a common convergence, although usually from paths that originated from very conflicting and dissimilar origins. Thus, extremely opposing viewpoints are oftentimes more similar than first glance might suggest, with distinct commonalty found within their final product. Throughout history, most scientific theory and discovery has seemed to be at odds, or at times even contrary to religious dogma and teachings. However that definitely does not imply that science is the enemy of religion.

Rather, the accumulation of scientific theory explaining our physical world has simply involved an evolution of knowledge and understanding over time. Such an evolution correspondingly requires periodic refinement of spiritual understanding, without necessarily implying that past doctrine was entirely incorrect. Indeed, such doctrine may only require minor revisions or certain reassessments in order to reflect the inclusion of all known scientific facts, including new technological discoveries.

The understanding between religion and science must constantly evolve. Both disciplines must be open and receptive to new thoughts and discoveries. While science attempts to explain our physical world, religion tends to describe and explain the spiritual realm. That inevitable mortal transition or release from the physical to the spiritual plane tends to connect both of those domains.

6

Humankind tends to think in terms of absolutes. Perhaps both the dimensions of spiritual and physical reality possess exceptions and contradictions within their own unique natural order. Consequently, scientific theory might always continue to conflict with religious belief, just as the paranormal conflicts with science. The ultimate truth might lie somewhere between, within some new concept yet to be explored. Regardless, at final conclusion, all living beings can simply be grouped into two categories: those who do not know what happens after physical death, and those who are unaware that they do not know what happens after physical death.

But if there exists no utopian heaven with streets of gold where all our desires are met, or abyss of hell where only pain and suffering is our constant companion, then where do we go? What actually happens to each of us at the time of physical death? We hear that we make our own heaven or hell right here on Earth. We have all observed those who seemingly lead a self-destructive life, as well as others with an outwardly charmed existence, with elements from both groups apparently defying both nature and explanation. But what if heaven and hell are only nebulous concepts, merely a personal state of mind?

The mind is the most powerful tool humans possess. It can be our worst enemy or our best friend. Each of us can create hardship or despair from any obstacle or event we encounter in life, or produce a positive and meaningful experience from that very same incident. The actual result being solely dependent upon how we view, accept, and respond toward each of those very same occurrences when ultimately experienced.

We can rationalize anything into acceptance, or overlook and avoid any thought or action we choose not to accept. If one dwells on a certain belief system or aspect of life only from a narrow perspective, their conviction can become real and all consuming, even if totally incorrect or merely

7

imagined. Such unenlightened believers can then skew all other perceptions to support and accommodate their central fabrication. As such falsehoods are perpetuated and remain fully embraced, reality becomes altered, allowing one's skewed perspectives to create delusions. We can literally force anything into 'existence' within our mind, while never actually altering the true reality that surrounds all of us. Such delusions then become completely real and tangible within that believer's false perception.

Any situation that is encountered in life may provide either a positive or negative outcome. Essentially one's thoughts, actions, attitudes, and perspectives that are employed to deal with any situation will become for each individual their ally or enemy. A disturbing or taxing event may be viewed detrimentally, resulting in defeat or failure; or it can be approached more positively as a learning experience, drawing upon one's best efforts to eventually emerge from such a negative and unpleasant encounter with a worthy outcome. To that degree, we do indeed create our own heaven or hell right here on Earth. But that awareness still does not provide finite answers as to what actually occurs at the time of physical death, or the ability of our essence to transcend such bodily demise, if indeed such a subsequent event might actually take place.

Then what does happen when life ceases to exist within our physical bodies? Is that the end? Our consciousness stops, our bodies decay, and we are forgotten except for a granite carving in a mowed field, or the presentation of flowers annually on Memorial Day? That does not appear to be a very imaginative Master Plan. It seemingly lacks fairness, without gain from one's untapped potential or realization of a 'bigger picture' that adds to some grand purpose of life. Are we all not left with some regrets from our past, with deeds we have yet to 'set right' or atone for, all while still possessing some unfinished goals awaiting completion sometime during our future? Is it even possible to

8

lead a truly 'perfect life' while trapped by our human frailties? Where is the line drawn that one person just 'makes-the-mark' to gain access into heaven, while another, with just one more unkind word spoken in life, burns in hell? Life must involve a much greater level of fairness and justice than that.

Should our environment, by mere chance of birth, dictate our trials and challenges throughout life, and thus influence our chance for hereafter happiness? The protected 'chosen few' who seldom face adversity, and thus any tough choices, would seem destined for an easier life style and path towards salvation. Such lives would certainly appear to have more ready access to an afterlife reward. Conversely, the highly exposed 'disadvantaged class,' who constantly encounter the toughest of life's challenges and its hardest roads, would certainly have more to overcome in order to even dream of such final utopia. Pure chance of birth or 'luck of the draw' should have nothing to do with one's destiny. A mere product of genetics or "there but for the grace of God" is certainly not a fair and just doctrine or Master Plan, nor does it provide for some greater grand purpose within physical life.

Discarding the more conventional approaches and belief systems that exist within our modern society as lacking in fairness and wisdom, to what other philosophies can we turn? While I profess no insight or vision into the hereafter, if indeed one actually exists, the concept of reincarnation simply makes the most sense to me. One in which luck, chance, environment, and genetics play no part other than as individual life-lessons. Those life-events and challenges simply provide potential learning experiences, wherein each of us controls our own destiny through personal actions we choose to implement toward those intended encounters.

Mortal life-paths always offer a physical existence where ultimate fairness is universal, with each and every soul required to overcome essentially the same obstacles during an unspecified cycle of incarnation within some specific life existence. Mastering those universal trials allows eventual obtainment of eternal tranquillity. These 'common' life-path events are provided over and over until their lessons are eventually learned, and personal character changes are made. Such continuous physical existences allow our choice-of-actions to ultimately dictate the final outcome from those encountered events.

Every incarnated life can provide the reward of personal growth through correction of one's faults, thus providing ensuing personal enlightenment. Or it can hold the price of stagnation by living an unproductive life that merely wastes time and opportunity. Each of us may choose either contentment from our successes, or suffering from our failures, based on our ultimate responses toward each of those lessons we encounter during successive life experiences.

Chapter Two

Intent

The belief in reincarnation has been proposed, disputed, propagated, repudiated, and debated countless times over the ages. This writing is not intended to be a comprehensive study, nor an attempt to prove the validity of this concept or its reality. Rather, this book provides only a basic introduction that exposes this belief as a way-of-life. Reincarnation is a rather elementary rationalization concerning the underlying meaning and purpose of life, as well as a simplistic explanation for the seemingly complex and inconsistent ways in which certain things happen, and why others do not. It is also why bad things do indeed happen to essentially good people, while those deserving punishment may seemingly evade their just retribution entirely, at least during present life.

Understanding the concept of reincarnation can often serve as a guide to everyday living by offering meaning and purpose to each action; through self discipline, understanding, correction, and the accumulation of knowledge. Such characteristics can help shape our actions and perhaps our very essence or composition throughout life, as well as any future lives we might live.

At the conclusion of physical existence, what if one could retain the 'good' accomplished and review the 'bad,' thus allowing for an additional chance to set things right? That would allow each of us to learn from past mistakes, correct any retained deficiencies, change bad habits, and improve our 'core self.' Such a premise is the very essence of the reincarnation belief. It is a building block approach,

11

wherein one builds upon a foundation of corrected prior deficiencies that have been overcome or replaced with positive traits, while seeking to add to one's ever changing stack of 'blocks,' repairing any cracked or weak ones during that ongoing process.

Such a building and improving process continues life-after-life, without having to go back and reset a new 'foundation' each time, but rather shoring-up any 'weak' blocks within existing ones, with the opportunity to continually add new ones. The opportunity always exists to increase one's strong foundation or destroy it, depending upon our attitudes, thoughts, and actions. The choice is left to each individual. It is a cumulative process from existence to existence, with no recognizable beginning due to constant change, or conceivable end due to everlasting life.

It is an eternity of successive experiences involving learning and correction; all intended to produce incremental growth towards ultimate perfection. Each successive life becomes one's stepping stone toward further progress. Such stepping stones are used to traverse life's purpose, starting from a neutral initiation and continuing through many subsequent lives of learning and correction, all leading towards the ultimate goal of perfection, resulting in eventual reunification with our Creator.

It is a journey taken with measured purpose toward the desired goal of perfection, allowing reabsorption by the Creator. Each journey's length, direction, happiness, hardships, rewards, and regrets are totally within one's control through our utilization of free will choice; regardless if it is evident to one's conscious-self or not. Physical death merely permits a change in 'vehicles,' providing each individual with a new and rejuvenated body, which can then be used to transverse that continuing journey. Such travel will not end until one reaches their final destination or goal of perfection. The beloved British poet, Robert Browning (1812-1889), seemed to imply such a continuance beyond the grave when he stated, "No work begun shall ever pause for death."[1] Such a continuing journey is everyone's mission in life, through which one's ultimate character is forged.

One initial reaction, indeed dismay, in returning for another physical life pertains to the logic (or lack thereof) in having to 'relearn' all the 'basics,' such as the alphabet, language, math tables, or other similar tangible concepts. As a rebuttal, what if one had previously learned the 'wrong' things, including incorrect facts, information, and untruths?

Prior lives may have involved many incorrect contemporary teachings, such as a flat Earth configuration where the sun and stars revolved around our planet; as well as other prior falsehoods that have since been repudiated. Perhaps successive 'knowledge' that might be learned during some 'future life' could prove certain present beliefs to be equally incorrect, as new discoveries and resultant understanding ultimately emerge.

We merely have to look at the world of medicine and the physical sciences as prime examples of how quickly contemporary truths can be repudiate (or conversely endured), with new theorems and hypotheses constantly being introduced. Consider the example of Humoral Theory, the curative medical technique practiced by physicians for more than two thousand years. That classic treatment involved the purging of fluids from an ill body, utilizing chemical blistering, leeches, or mechanical 'cupping' in an attempt to balance the patient's 'vital liquid levels.' Such past practices are now shunned, just as today's leading breakthroughs may some day be viewed as primitive twentieth and early twenty first century 'absurdities.'

If reincarnation is the mechanism for continuance of our individual essence, then why do we not remember anything from our past lives? Essentially, all 'prior' knowledge must be blocked, so one may grow as an individual, independent of past mistakes, untruths, or prior ingrained 'bad' habits. Past memory must be blocked so its recall would not influence one's present actions and responses to current occurrences, when encountered during that incarnation.

Certainly, any previously learned falsehoods and 'carry-over' undesirable traits would serve as impediments to our present and future growth. Since this memory blocking process can not be a discriminating or selective one, all prior data must be suppressed or blocked, so as not to unduly influence future character development. Moreover, the human mind presently appears to be incapable of handling the flood of data reflecting all past lives while encountering one's present life.

Additionally, 'prior' knowledge could occasionally hinder or prevent 'future' knowledge, thereby creating an obstacle for present and future progress. Typically, new innovations and thought processes often blossom from 'ignorance' of what 'can not' be done. To some extent, a fresh new approach, unencumbered by perceived conventions and limitations, often spawns new leading-edge discoveries. Furthermore, one's prior language and alphabet may be of little use, if reborn into a 'foreign culture.'

Yet specific indications occasionally exist, which suggest certain 'skilled' traits might be carried over from life to life. Such an occurrence may become evident with a child *protégé*, such as the untrained musician able to 'play-by-ear,' the 'natural' or 'born' athlete, or the mechanically inclined. Some have wondered why certain students seem to easily grasp 'new' teachings, while many of their contemporaries struggle for similar comprehension. Minimally, such unexplained but 'gifted exceptions' certainly hint at some previous exposure to specifically acquired talents or past enhancement of certain skills or attributes.

That might suggest that some part of our past existence continues into the realm beyond physical death, and is at least partially retained when reborn into a subsequent incarnation. Yet physical death remains an unknown commodity, with equally unknown consequences. However, there does appear

14

to be some documented phenomena that have been noted at the time of certain medically declared death. Substantial clinical data have been generated concerning the so-called 'after-death' or 'near-death' experience (aka NDE). These occurrences deal with people who have been diagnosed as 'clinically dead' by recognized medical experts, yet came back to life after claiming to have experienced a brief existence, phase of consciousness, or 'strange journey' into another realm or spiritual domain before eventually being revived.

Perhaps the earliest recorded NDE was made by an 18th century French military doctor, Pierre-Jean du Monchaux, in 1740, which was subsequently published in the *Anecdotes de Médecine*. That olden account was later 'rediscovered' within a second-hand copy of that 'antique' medical book, which had been purchased by Dr. Philippe Charlier, a modern medical doctor and archaeologist.[2] It was Dr. Charlier who recognized the 'symptoms' described in that 18th century account as a NDE. The patient further recalled that he never had a "nicer moment," which seemed to compare to an even earlier account made by a 12th century theologian. That olden Church authority had previously claimed that at the moment approaching the dissolution of our body and soul, the soul is lit by a "*luminositas lucis primae*" (a primary light ray).[3]

Supposedly during such a NDE, affected individuals may have experienced another separate and distinct realm of consciousness. The reported modern similarities of these experiences, as compiled from many different case studies, tend to suggest the existence of some form of continuation of 'consciousness' within an unknown, remarkable, and thought-provoking realm. Some commonly experienced occurrences encountered during such 'near-death' experiences include:

1. Floating-out from one's physical body.
2. The viewing of one's own body as a detached spectator, usually from above.
3. An overwhelming sense of great peace, warmth, and

wholeness.

4. The continuance of one's consciousness, including full thought processes and memory.
5. The absence of any pain or physical limitations.
6. Travel through a 'tunnel,' accompanied by a sense of another presence, perhaps a 'guide' or master, while apparently 'traveling' with that 'companion' for some distance.
7. A lack of fear, accompanied with reassurance of a natural order unfolding as destined.
8. An awareness of a bright light, which provided great comfort, calm, and warmth.
9. A review of events from the just-completed life, as a form of self-assessment.
10. A strong desire to stay within that ethereal realm.
11. A realization that such a spiritual realm is accessible by all souls, not just for people of a certain select religion, 'saintly' people, or merely some specific 'chosen' group.
12. Being informed of one's inability to remain within this realm, since intended purpose or allotted time planned for the present physical life had not yet been fulfilled.
13. Displeasure with having to return back to one's physical body.
14. Profound change within one's outlook towards life after returning to the physical state.
15. Subsequent lack of fear toward the inevitable future death of one's physical body.

It is interesting to note that this phenomenon, at least to some degree, has been observed, studied, and documented through scientific empirical means. During the early 20th century, the noted neurosurgeon Wilder Graves Penfield attempted to fully map the human brain. Dr. Penfield ultimately discovered that certain emotional and physical (muscular) functions resided in separate locations within the brain. Clinically controlled research deep within the right temporal lobe was conducted by Dr. Penfield, which involved precise electrical stimulation within that region of the brain. His extensive experimentation reproduced the ability to duplicate the most common effects and experiences of the 'near-death' phenomenon, except for the presence of the 'bright light' and its comforting and reassuring ability.

Science has attempted to discredit, discount, or explain these 'near-death' encounters with numerous rationalizations, concluding that such 'unusual' experiences were simply the result of one or more of the following conditions:

1. Oxygen deprivation.
2. Hallucinations.
3. Wish fulfillment.
4. An unconscious fantasy.
5. The influence of religious beliefs.
6. A direct result of physical trauma.

A study released in 2007 by researchers at the University of Kentucky theorized that the out-of-body phenomenon also associated with the near death experience may be caused by disturbances within the brain that affect the body's arousal system. This function regulates the various states of consciousness between phases of sleep and full wakefulness. Such brain abnormalities can blend the various states of awareness into each another, rather than allowing passage directly from REM sleep into normal wakefulness. This blending of different states might account for some abnormal conditions such as sleep paralysis, as well as certain audio and visual hallucinations.[4]

While such accounts, experiments, and explanations do not conclusively prove or refute a continuation of the human consciousness after physical death, they do suggest a strong possibility of at least a temporary continuance of our essence.

17

That essence is the nebulous commodity that represents the distinct but intangible elements of each individual, which extends beyond one's physical existence, and apparently differentiates each of us from everyone else within the confines of a finite physical time frame. That essence apparently has both a physical and ethereal component and reality. A Gallup Poll conducted in the 1990s found that seventy percent of the United States population believed in some form of life-after-death.

Additionally, overwhelming paranormal evidence supports the probability of another dimension, perhaps the existence of a spiritual plane, one in which our consciousness may be compatible. Although purely speculative, such an 'other-side of reality' might be a parallel universe, a plane of higher consciousness, an inter-dimensional realm consisting of different frequencies or vibrational rates, a displacement in time, or any number of other phenomena that may be beyond humanity's present comprehension. The explanation and nature of such a realm is moot, since our present basis of reality is confined only within the known physical world.

Modern science has demonstrated that when our physical senses are blocked or impeded, we lose all reference with our surroundings or environment. Without physical references, one can no longer be sure of any tangible reality. Perhaps the physical world 'blocks' the reality of that spiritual realm, which might presently but 'unknowingly' surround us, revealing that 'other-side' only when impediments within our physical world are 'removed' after corporeal death.

The possibility of a spiritual realm seems plausible, considering the accumulated amount of paranormal incidents such as 'near-death' experiences; out-of-body phenomena; incidents of *déjà vu*; regressive-hypnosis accounts; documented clinical case studies suggesting reincarnation; and indications of retained talent carry-over; as well as numerous other similar occurrences. If such minimal tangible evidence provides some credibility for the existence of a spiritual plane, it does not favor the concept of a religious heaven or hell belief over the notion of a spiritual world where one's consciousness goes between rebirths after death, or *vice versa*. It merely suggests a new spiritual dimension that is unseen, unexplained, and unknown to our physical consciousness.

Such phenomena also lend credibility to the belief that humankind is comprised of two distinct parts: a physical element, the body; and a spiritual element, the soul. Such a belief supports the philosophical theory of dualism, which combines the compatible commodities of matter and spirit, forming both the natural and the supernatural. The widely held belief in dualism is fundamental to numerous religious doctrines including Zoroastrianism and Cartesianism.

Zoroastrianism proclaimed the existence of opposing forces of Good and Evil, while the theory of Cartesianism proposed that the whole of reality is made up of two classes of substance: thinking substance or 'mind,' and extended substance or body. That belief is directly based on the interpretation of views expressed by the renowned French philosopher and scientist, René Descartes (1596-1650), who is considered the 'father of modern philosophical inquiry.' Such a pairing of body and soul suggests a certain dual reliance or connection; perhaps an association previously described in the writings of Edmund Spenser (1552-1559), when he stated: "For of the soul the body form doth take; for soul is form, and doth the body make."[5]

While the physical unit of one's existence seemingly can not survive without the spiritual part, it would appear that the spiritual component continues to exist, at least temporarily beyond its corporeal existence, after the death of its physical element. It was Horace (65-8 BC), the Roman lyricist, who stated, "I shall not all together die,"[6] furthering such a belief. The concept of an immortal soul is not testable within the material world, but presumably can be verified or refuted after mortal death. However, such obtainable and positive

19

proof does pose certain obvious limitations for any researcher or author seeking to report on its ultimate validity and verification; as would the subsequent problem of how to convey such findings back to the physical realm after corporeal death, once they were ultimately revealed.

As previously stated, I profess no insight into this spiritual realm, or profound personal experience with the 'near-death' phenomenon. Nor do I claim to have had any life-altering mystic encounters, nor even tangible *déjà vu* flashes. My personal conviction with the belief in reincarnation arises from 'bits-and-pieces' that have been exposed to me through deep personal introspection, throughout various periods during my life. Eventually, with enough 'bits' the 'pieces' began to fit together as within a puzzle. The individual elements made little sense until finally fitted together into the 'whole picture.' The conviction of continuing cycles of incarnation then materialized when those combined elements became clear, revealing reincarnation's underlying fairness, elegant simplicity, and supreme brilliance.

Such a conclusion simply made more sense than any other philosophy pertaining to life's purpose. It is the very essence of simplistic clarity, supplying answers to all the mysteries of life. It is interesting to note that the many accomplishments of Galileo Galilei (1564-1642), the Italian inventor, physicist, and astronomer, involved very little actual experimentation. Most of his discoveries were based primarily on common sense and reasoning. Galileo held the conviction that every correct theory would have a simple and natural explanation.

Once the concept of reincarnation is embraced, unorthodox thoughts and attitudes might emerge that seem quite dissimilar and unique from other belief systems. These unconventional traits include notions that might manifest in some of the following ways:

1. A finite feeling of contentment and comfort with the reincarnation belief. Essentially, if this belief system were to be proven wrong, no change would be made to the way life was being lived, as it relates to the way-of-life implemented by following this concept.

2. There exists no desire to convert others, or force this belief system upon others; merely a desire to expose this philosophy as an alternate concept for open-minded consideration.

3. A conviction that reincarnation offers ultimate fairness, justice, and meaning, along with purpose toward a finite goal. A belief that 'what we sow, we also reap,' either now or in some lifetime to come. That every individual must face and overcome essentially the same obstacles at some point during continuing and successive physical lives. Those learning their 'lessons' by overcoming retained deficiencies and gaining enlightenment simply need not repeat those unpleasant tests over and over.

4. The realization that who and what we are today, as distinct individuals, is the total result and product of our past. That our prior lives have shaped the very nature and character of our present self. Thus, no reason exists to blame others or a difficult past, or become a 'martyr' burdened with self-pity; since our present composition is the direct result of how we handled and dealt with every prior event ever experienced. We simply created our own suffering or successes in life, while always controlling our ultimate fate.

5. That the promise of a reward or punishment is poor motivation in policing humanity's actions. Rather, Confucius' *Golden Rule* of 'doing unto others...' could replace all manmade laws and religious commandments, if everyone would simply follow its intent, thereby producing universal harmony.

21

Chapter Three

History

The concept of reincarnation is not new. A thorough review of Earth's past reveals its ancient roots as arguably the oldest 'spiritual belief' on Earth. Modern anthropologists have detected a metaphysical aspect that was an integral part of humanity's earliest body of knowledge; a prehistoric collection that is generally referred to in modern times as the *Ancient Wisdom*. That archaic knowledge included a primitive awareness of a superior order to which all matter in the universe is constantly subjected. According to tradition, adhering to this intended plan created harmony throughout the universe. This same archaic understanding was further associated with the concept of human immortality, which was connected with the belief in reincarnation.

Professor Cornelius Loew recognized that this prehistoric concept endured over the ages, continuing into much later times in ancient Mesopotamia when it was known as the cosmological conviction; a connection with a Cosmic Order that existed throughout the universe and permeated every level of reality. However, recognition of that concept during Mesopotamian times was of a profound awareness that man had not adhered to that formerly established divine model, which had previously integrated organization, proper human attitudes, and relationships into daily life.[1] Thus, the resultant departure from man's prior observance of this sacred order necessitated an annual Renewal Tradition, which required humanity to seek regeneration after a year of decline, thereby assuring the revitalization of life.[2]

From that initial and most basic prehistoric concept,

many of Earth's earliest religious beliefs emerged. A review of those olden religious doctrines reveals a consistent pattern of continuous distortion and change from that original universal concept, since first being revealed or imparted to humankind. Such ongoing alterations can be recognized from later attributes that were first associated with the 'snake,' which originally symbolized the process of reincarnation through its shedding process when its skin was discarded, once again becoming renewed. Since primordial times, the snake had been associated with wisdom and knowledge, but only later was denigrated into a symbol of evil.

It is believed that pre-flood humans comprehended a concept for the continuation of each individual consciousness after physical death, which was accompanied by ascension through or into a different non-corporeal dimension where each consciousness reintegrated or mingled with other lifeforces or similar entities. From such a realm, subsequent physical existences were chosen, ones that would provide further learning opportunities from which each individual consciousness could gain enlightenment, thus perfecting their character composition in a step by step fashion. Hence, the seemingly overwhelming task of perfection is spread over as many physical lifetimes as needed, without 'pressure' of failure ever dissuading such a lofty pursuit.

Furthermore, the earliest detectable spiritual concept of existence held by primitive humans was one that reflected a belief in only a finite animation of each physical body. That belief was accompanied by an inference that some type of non-physical life force was associated with each consciousness. Such an unseen commodity, known in those ancient records as the *Inner Man*,[3] continued to exist after physical death through the human soul, which then inhabited an unseen realm.

Such a belief is the very essence of reincarnation. A corruption of its basic concept occurred through a degradation and distortion of its original understanding by later human priests, who then created numerous imagined afterlife 'lands,' either of a paradise or an atrocity, to which each deceased entity might travel. That notion was perpetuated over the millennia, and further altered into the generally accepted belief that only the immortal soul or spirit, the essence of each individual, survives the physical death of its containment vessel, its body. It is only that non-corporeal component or 'essential consciousness' that reunites with the Creator within the spiritual realm, perhaps in some unknown pure energy form.

The oldest known religious belief is described as that of the Mother Goddess, traced back to the Cro-Magnons of the Gravettian period as early as 24,000 BC. Such veneration may not have been a true religious belief, but rather an honor focused on female fertility reflecting childbirth capability. Another possibility may be the reverence bestowed upon a female leader, perhaps within a matriarchal society. Much later evidence of Mother Goddess veneration was found at Tell Mureybut (modern day Aleppo, Syria), which dated to *c*.8000 BC. Both the Mother Goddess and the competing Bull god cult were subsequently worshipped in Catal Hüyük around 7000 BC. The earliest indications of a Fish or Water god were then detected in Europe around 5450 BC, and also later in Mesopotamia as early as *c*.4900 BC.

Substantial evidence exists to indicate that most ancient people believed in the reincarnation of the soul. Colonel James Churchward and W. Raymond Drake, authors and researchers of ancient civilizations and their records, have both claimed that the earliest recognized religious belief was that of reincarnation.[4] In ancient India and Tibet, it was thought to be the mechanism that allowed each soul to choose the time and place for its rebirth, during a time period when cosmic influences and unfolding events would provide specific lessons for the evolution of that specific soul.[5] This theory, as well as any other religious concept, seemingly would not have been a self-evident belief conceived by

25

'primitive' but developing people, and thus would indicate its origin as an imparted concept or 'wisdom' derived from more enlightened or 'divine beings.'

Such a reincarnation process apparently also included the metempsychosis or transmigration (aka metamorphosis) belief that originated with the much later Egyptians as well as the Hindus of India. That reincarnation doctrine is further connected with the deficit-or-dividend concept of *karma*. Karma is the inevitable sequence of events that emanate from every action, referring to the consequences that result from every deed committed within the physical universe.

The Christian theologian and ecclesiastic writer, Quintus Tertullian (160-230 AD), stated that the teachings of the Egyptian god Thoth included the doctrine of reincarnation. Such ancient teachings were associated with the even older original religion of Osiris, which was taught to the human civilizations that existed before the Great Flood. Much of the teachings of Thoth are only known from the scant fragments written by the third century BC Egyptian scribe and high priest, Manetho, which were later preserved by the monk, Georgios Syncellus, around *c*.800 AD. It is known that Thoth's teachings included numerous reincarnation facts pertaining to an individual's essence (their consciousness or soul). His teachings further divulged humanity's innate ability to ultimately recognize or comprehend such metaphysical truths through individual self-realization.

Other Egyptian records also professed reincarnation doctrine, such as the obscure text that author and researcher James Churchward identified as the *Papyrus of Anana*. Anana reportedly was the Chief Scribe and personal counsel to Pharaoh Seti II of the XIX Dynasty. According to the *c*.1205 BC Egyptian *Papyrus of Anana*: "Men do not live once only and then depart...they live many times in many places, although not always on this world. Between each life there is a veil of darkness. The doors will open at last, and show us all the chambers through which our feet have

26

wandered from the beginning."[6]   Such an olden Egyptian concept claimed that each physical body was mortal, while its soul, called the *Ka* (also *Khu* or *Kw*), was immortal. However, during physical life this *Ka* was subordinate to the free will choice possessed by every human.[7]

The reincarnation process was recognized during ancient times as the accepted underlying mechanism that provided immortality to humankind. This ethereal process allowed for an eternal continuation or existence of one's consciousness, during which the imperishability of each soul was ultimately revealed, exposing its dual nature wherein its compatibility was shown to exist within both the spiritual and physical realms.

The ancient Egyptian religious belief declared that only the soul ascended into heaven to live with the 'gods.' They knew with certainty that a decaying mortal body could not survive physical death. But the Egyptians also believed that it was absolutely necessary to preserve the deceased physical body as well as humanly possible. Sir E. A. Wallis Budge, the noted Egyptologist, concluded that such a belief was a form of 'insurance policy,' allowing the deceased and their families a 'double assurance' of the departed soul's entrance into heaven.[8]

Egyptologist Donald A. Mackenzie revealed his detection of two different religious beliefs that apparently were prevalent throughout archaic Egypt.   One belief followed the original concept of reincarnation spread by Osiris, while a rival belief "from the east" taught worship of humanlike gods.[9]   Those two rival concepts apparently existed intermittently, each exuding its influence at various times over both Upper and Lower Egypt, until finally being united around 3150 BC under King Menes. Such a change in ancient Egyptian ideology reflects one of the earliest examples in which the reincarnation concept was altered by a subsequent religious belief.

Similar concepts paralleling the earliest beliefs of the

ancient Egyptians were also apparent in contemporaneous ancient India, which had a richly established religious belief of its own and, along with Egypt, perhaps the one most closely following the oldest concepts that were associated with the original reincarnation doctrine. Their established belief was later called Hinduism, although with certain known changes from its original version. Hinduism references no founder of its religious doctrine, believing it to be both 'eternal and ageless.' As with later Egyptian concepts, Hinduism beliefs were also subsequently altered to suit humanity's desires and perceptions, commencing with the earliest Aryan intrusion into India around 3000 BC.

The most notable changes occurred during the earliest instances of alteration and distortion, when physical humanlike 'gods' were first introduced. However, the earliest record of a specific humanlike divinity was found in Mesopotamia with the Sumerian god Enki, who dates to at least 3350 BC. A true religious belief in the Godhead or a pantheon of gods then first emerged within the ancient culture of Sumer (aka Sumeria) around *c*.3150 BC, wherein specific physical superhuman beings were worshipped or venerated. Similar superhumanlike 'gods' were also incorporated into the Hindu and Egyptian pantheons about or shortly after that same time frame. The humanlike gods of ancient mythology and epics then dominated religious beliefs during the ensuing millennia.

However, vestiges from the earlier original reincarnation concept can still be detected in many other ancient religions, preserving much of its basic original doctrine. Around 2000 BC, the Hebrew faith emerged under their patriarch Abraham, although their ancestry dated back much further, long before the Great Flood, with its 'Adam-to-Noah' lineage. During that earlier lineage, a divine being reportedly created a paradise in which numerous gifts and instructions were bestowed upon those first humans, with certain servitude duties expected in return. Yet the Hebrew *Book of Splendor*, the *Zohar*, also includes reincarnation beliefs. It states: "If a soul is planted here below and fails to arrive at its best, it is withdrawn and planted again on Earth until it is perfected and able to attain to the sixth heaven from which it came."[10]

The ancient Greek religion also worshipped physical gods, ones similar in concept to the Sumerian and Egyptian beliefs, although a philosophical awakening, one as early as the 8th century BC, resurrected certain *Ancient Wisdom* teachings. A reemergence of the reincarnation belief then followed, which resurfaced with still further additional alterations and changes. However, the ancient Greeks' knew that only an individual's spiritual component, their soul, survived death; not its physical body. They believed that the soul is not a physical commodity, but merely a single dimensional point, one without spatial size or properties. Plato believed that the universe was divinely created, and that all physical creations everywhere within the universe also shared in the similar concept of an immortal soul.[11]

It becomes evident that the body of knowledge known as the *Ancient Wisdom*, which reportedly was bestowed by an ancient Divinity upon Earth during archaic times, contained some form of Sacred Knowledge that was also known as the Tree of Knowledge or the Tree of Life. Perhaps the Creator had previously revealed such esoteric facts pertaining to our physical universe and the purpose of physical existence to some prior otherworldly species that had ultimately obtained higher divine enlightenment. That species may have later bestowed such knowledge upon early humankind. Or perhaps the Creator allowed such knowledge to be retained and remembered by select and highly enlightened souls that subsequently reincarnated on Earth in order to divulge such wisdom and revelations to their human contemporaries.

Regardless of its source, ancient humanity seemed consumed with a metaphysical belief or reverence that connected the physical world with an unseen spiritual realm. The basic concept of creation and its Supreme Creator permeated the traditions and cultures of many ancient human societies. That initial religious concept reflected a belief in only a finite physical life, with the continuation of each consciousness through man's soul, its *Inner Man*, which survived corporeal death to inhabit some unseen ethereal realm.

Since reincarnation was revealed to archaic humans as an element of the *Ancient Wisdom* knowledge, it certainly is not new; with its concept recognized as the oldest original spiritual belief. Such a core belief has typically been an integral part of most Eastern religions, with its later introduction into the Western world by the Greek philosopher, Pythagoras (582-507 BC), in the sixth century BC. Pythagoras was one of the most widely known, although later educators, in this spread of esoteric teachings and religious concepts through his own Mystery School.

Around 530 BC, Pythagoras moved to a Greek colony in Crotona, Italy, where he taught classes at a college located there. His teachings were based on esoteric Egyptian wisdom, with lessons in mathematics and the physical sciences reportedly based on some secretive 'lost' knowledge, which considered 'numbers' to be the essence and principle of all things. Pythagoras also formulated his own dogma that eventually evolved into a theological belief that survived his death, which was later subsequently promoted by his many devoted followers.

Pythagoras believed he was the reincarnation of Euphorbus, the son of Panthus, a warrior in the Trojan War who was killed by a spear from Menalaus.[12] His new theology, known as the Pythagorean Movement, was blended into a religious belief professing the transmigration of the soul, along with the belief in a mathematical basis or relationship that was employed uniformly throughout the physical universe, one in which all natural laws were followed and obeyed.

That belief was supposedly based on Orphism, a mystical

religious belief derived from the writings of the musician and poet, Orpheus. Orphism is known from sixth century BC writings made by his later followers, found buried with them in their graves. That belief focused around the god Dionysus Zagreus, the reported son of Zeus and Persephone. It was a belief in the dualism of human weakness towards evil, and the 'divine element' also present in man. Mortals, such as humankind, were required to live a long series of reincarnated lives, through which they could eventually eliminate all their evil faults, resulting in complete liberation and a reunification with the Creator. Orphism professed that humans had an immortal soul that was released or freed from the physical body upon death, to reinhabit an ethereal realm where the soul remained until inhabiting its next mortal body. When the soul was eventually 'purified' from all faults and character deficiencies, that soul then returned to its source for final reunification with the Creator.

The age during which Pythagoras lived was a unique period in Earth history, during which an explosion of new or 'revised' philosophical and religious thought occurred. Such a period is remarkable for its emergence of a number of new religions, which included several offshoots of the Hindu religion, such as Jainism and Buddhism.

Jainism theology professes a belief in an immortal soul, which is considered to be a formless, eternal, and independently conscious entity. Jainism professes that an infinite number of souls exist, with reincarnation as the process through which each soul obtains its physical vessel or body. That soul pervades the whole vessel, assuming the size and shape of each individual body. When released from the physical vessel due to bodily death, the soul severs all connection with that body, and reverts to its eternal 'spiritual form' composition, one that exists within the unseen ethereal realm.

Each soul passes through two phases, a bound state and a free state. The bound state occurs during physical life, or a series of numerous lives, during which the soul attempts to conquer its deficiencies. During those 'temporary' phases, the soul possesses differing levels or degrees of imperfections. Any retention of faults from one physical life to the next is due to incorrect and perverse beliefs, which includes 'blind convictions.' The 'freed state' finally occurs at the end of the reincarnation cycle, when the condition known as 'perfect bliss' has been obtained, which is considered to be everyone's ultimate or ideal goal. That ethereal 'freed state' is the natural state of each consciousness, and the one sought as a permanent state. It is achieved over a series of numerous physical life times of learning, correcting imperfections and faults, thereby obtaining a perfected state of bliss as the ultimate objective.

Buddhism also professes a reincarnation belief, which includes the transmigration process, a continuation or renewed cycle of rebirth that is based on acquired karma from prior actions. It is through such karma that all past and ongoing lives are ultimately connected. While Buddhism believes in karma, it does not recognize an immortal soul. The ultimate goal of its followers is to seek enlightenment, thereby reaching Nirvana, a state of total enlightenment and liberation from physical temptation, a state of spiritual purity. Elimination of such character deficiencies allows the return of each entity to its source, the Creator, with the absorption of such perfected entities by the Creator, thus losing the individuality of each essence. In contrast, the earlier Hindu belief states that an essence's individual identity continues to remain after unification with the Creator.

Yet another devout ancient belief first emerged in ancient Persia, and solidified into a formal religion also during the 6th century BC. The Persian prophet Zoroaster (aka Zarathustra) started a new religious belief known as Zoroastrianism in *c.*625 BC after he began receiving revelations from the god Ahura Mazda [Lord Wisdom]. Those revelations were formed into a doctrine that was recorded as psalms or *Gathas*, which later produced a major portion of the sacred scripture known as the *Avesta*. Zoroaster was one of the first prophets to preach monotheism, along with a dualism of opposing pairs, such as Truths and Lies, or Good and Evil.

Zoroastrianism priests, called Magi, employed extremely ethical laws, based upon a highly intellectual dispensation of rules, justice, intent, devotion, integrity, and morality. Its doctrine is best described as a 'cause and effect' religious belief, or a 'way of life.' This belief proposed an afterlife reward in a desirable spiritual 'paradise' realm, or a punishment in hell.

The Mithra cult is believed to be an offshoot, or perhaps a modified form of Zoroastrianism. According to certain accounts, Mithra was the son of the god Ahura Mazda. Ahura Mazda first appointed Mithra as 'a promptly-sacrificing, loud-chanting priest.' Many followers believed that Ahura Mazda eventually transferred his reign to Mithra and his wife, Anahita. Mithra was a 'god of contracts' who maintained law and order, punishing the wrong while defending the 'contract.' Mithra later became an equally important god of the Romans, whose reverence was spread by the legions of Roman soldiers across the Near East and the Mediterranean, while often competing with the then newly emerging Christian belief. Numerous theologians consider Mithraism to have been the most important Oriental religious influence on later Christianity, and perhaps the forerunner or nucleus for much of the ensuing Christian faith. The numerous similarities between Mithraism and Christianity caused St. Augustine to declare that the priests of Mithra apparently worshipped the same deity as St. Augustine himself.

Belief in reincarnation also proliferated throughout Greece, largely through the teachings of Plato (428-348 BC) during the fourth century BC. Plato, credited as the Athenian founder of Western philosophy, is widely considered to be the

'Western Father' of reincarnation doctrine.

Plato considered Socrates to be the ultimate philosopher. Socrates had taught reincarnation doctrine to Plato, stating that the soul is able to explore its own nature because it is illuminated with consciousness. Plato propagated the conviction that the soul participates in the eternal power that orders the cosmos. The Godhead, according to Plato, strove to direct the actions of man, bringing humanity into harmony with some Cosmic Symphony. It was also believed that man must work in harmony with such higher powers. Professor Cornelius Loew noted that the Greek Solon was the first man to interpret the premise that man was directly responsible for all order or disorder, with human actions linked with a cause and effect connection.[13] Causality is always the same, whether in nature or in man's actions, according to the ancient Greeks. They believed in a compensatory reaction of the cosmos against all of humanity's weaknesses and transgressions, essential professing a belief in 'karma' or some cosmic 'cause and effect.'

The later Roman poet and philosopher, Virgil, also advocated the concept of reincarnation. That act may have contributed to the rapid propagation of the belief in Mithraism throughout the early Roman Empire. The similarities between Mithraism and Christianity are startling. Both faiths believe in a messiah who was sacrificed as atonement for sin, along with a resurrection of the dead, followed by eternal life after a final judgment, with either a resultant reward in heaven or a punishment in hell. Other similarities include worship on Sunday, the Day of the Sun, in honor of the Sun god, rather than the Jewish Sabbath; celebrations through religious suppers; ethical standards or requirements; and baptism, although the followers of Mithra utilized the blood of a sacrificed bull rather than water.

Mithra was described as a dying-rising savior who had twelve disciples that represented the twelve signs of the Zodiac. He performed miracles such as raising the dead, healing the sick, making the blind see and the lame walk; with both Jesus and Mithra reportedly able to cast out devils. The pagan festival *Brumalia* was part of the celebration of Mithra's birthday on December 25, a time when shepherds, along with Persian Magi, had brought gifts to his sacred birthplace, the Cave of the Rock. Christianity eventually became the prominent religion throughout the Roman Empire, under Constantine's rule. It is accepted that Jesus had preached His belief in the concept of reincarnation and its accompanying doctrine. According to archaeologist Colonel James Churchward, an oral history was preserved that indicated Jesus was schooled in a Himalayan monastery over a period of 12 years. Eventually, during much later times, a written record was reportedly made in the Hemis Monastery at Leh, Kashmir, compiled from earlier oral traditions that had documented those studies by Jesus. According to those traditions, Jesus had reviewed the *Sacred Naacal Writings* and commented on them, claiming the Naacal records stated: "...it was not the material body of man that was reincarnated [not its previous original physical body]...but the soul or spirit only that was reincarnated."[14] Jesus reportedly made that declaration as a clarification to dispute certain 'monastery masters' who had been professing that both the soul and deceased physical body of an individual actually underwent the process of reincarnation.

Jesus' comments and teachings concerning reincarnation were also contained in many early writings and certain 'suppressed' gospels. However, nearly all Biblical references have since been removed. Some remaining New Testament passages, such as Matthew 17:10-13 and Luke 1:17, infer that the olden Hebrew prophet Elias (aka Elijah) had been reincarnated as John the Baptist.

References to those 'lost' or deleted gospels are known from the writings of respected 'olden' theologians and philosophers. According to the French philosopher Voltaire (aka François Marie Arouet, 1694-1778), who was educated

35

at a Catholic Jesuit college, much of Jesus' teachings were later rejected by the early Church. Voltaire wrote that: "By the end of the first century there were some thirty gospels, each belonging to a different society, and thirty sects of Christians had sprung up in Asia Minor, Syria, Alexandria, and even Rome."[15]

The removal of reincarnation doctrine from the Christian faith started with the earliest revisions to its original gospels, wherein documented redaction and distortions are known to have occurred. Such selective editing was evidently so thorough that Voltaire concluded that: "None of the early Fathers of the Church cited a single passage from the four gospels as we accept them today."[16] Voltaire also noted that those same early Church Fathers who failed to quote from the later 'original' gospels had ultimately included several passages that were found only in apocryphal gospels, which had otherwise been wholly rejected for canonization.[17]

The prolific writings of Origen (185-254 AD) attempted to preserve those original 30 gospels. St. Jerome (340-400 AD) exalted Origen as "...the greatest teacher of the Church since the Apostles."[18] His tenets are believed to have been based on accepted and true gospels that had existed during his life time. Many of his texts have since disappeared, eliminating much of his insight and knowledge from future generations. He firmly believed in reincarnation, relying on the teachings of Plato, Aristotle, and Jesus. In his *Contra Celsum*, he stated: "Is it not more in conformity with reason that every soul...is introduced into a body according to its desserts and former actions?"[19] He further stated: "The soul, which is immaterial and invisible in its nature, exists in no material place without having a body suited to the nature of that place."[20]

Origen, in his *De Principiis*, further stated: "Every soul...comes into this world strengthened by the victories or weakened by the defeats of its previous life. Its place in this world as a vessel appointed to honor or dishonor, is determined by its previous merits or demerits. Its work in this world determines its place in the world which is to follow this."[21]

The 'finalized' version of the Bible neither condemns the theory of reincarnation nor directly endorses it. The allusions to reincarnation left in the Bible are isolated, and at best fragmentary. As with other revisions made to the gospels, elimination of references to reincarnation can not be traced to any one date or event. Rather, they occurred over various periods of time, as the result of numerous different efforts. However, scattered records document that Jesus not only discussed cycles of recurring life, but also professed His apparent belief in the reincarnation process.

Some claim that the formal condemnation of reincarnation started with the First Ecumenical Council, which consisted of 300 religious leaders called together by Constantine in 325 AD. That meeting became known as the First Council of Nicaea, which cleverly removed any direct mention of reincarnation from the Bible, while leaving its references in the apocryphal texts. Reincarnation, which had been embraced by nearly all 'Ancient Religions' as well as the earliest Christian teachings, had survived for well over 4,000 years, until being further suppressed by the Roman Emperor Theodosius in 384 AD with strict edicts.

Later in 533 AD, Emperor Justinian then convened a local synod in Constantinople, along with a later universal Ecumenical Council in 553. Those gatherings were assembled as religious committees to decide on Church canon, but were actually intended to eliminate the doctrine of reincarnation and past lives. Those Church leaders cloaked that process in the form of religious reforms, with 'binding excommunication' ordered for any reincarnation advocate or follower, essentially decreeing reincarnation to be a heretical belief.

The doctrine put forth by the Monophysite sect of the early Christian Church attempted to discredit all references to reincarnation contained in the original gospels. Perhaps the final official action used to fully eradicate reincarnation from official Church doctrine emerged during the Fifth Ecumenical Congress in 553 AD. Convened in Constantinople, the Fifth Ecumenical Congress condemned all the writings of Origen, an act that firmly repudiated Origen's belief in reincarnation. The redaction of his writings effectively removed any remaining reincarnation vestige from official Church dogma.

Additional editing and revisions occurred in numerous other areas of early Church records. That fact is well documented in many scholarly works dealing with the Bible. The *Anecdota* (*Secret History*) by Procopius in *c*.535 AD, was written in the Greek language and protectively hidden away until the 19th century, when it was 'discovered' by a private collector in Rome.[22] It exposes the History of the Church under the Emperor Justinian (483-565) and his Empress Theodora (508-547); a period during which a substantial portion of Church history either vanished, or was greatly altered. That sixth century period included numerous councils, decrees, and edicts that altered prior doctrine and records professed by the early Church, while excluding teachings that stated the preexistence of the soul (and by implication, reincarnation) from the Christian creed, with the effect of further condemning the writings of Origen.

Some later efforts to reinstate the reincarnation belief, such as those employed by Manichaeism (which still later led to Catharism), acknowledged only the immortality of the soul through reincarnation. The Church viciously attacked all such movements. In 1208, Pope Innocent III declared a crusade against those sects, while the later Inquisition suppressed any remaining vestige of the reincarnation belief, which the Church had earlier professed as heresy. Not until the last half of the 19th century was the concept of reincarnation revived, and then only among philosophers, researchers, and a few fearless theologians.

A resemblance to the basic reincarnation belief can also

be found in the religion of the Hopi clan of the Pueblo Indians. Hopi belief states that beyond our present world, six more realms exist, marking our Road of Life.[23] In each life, man starts out pure (or more correctly 'neutral,' without 'new' blemishes or achievements). The world (our present life reality) either corrupts that life with evil, requiring yet another life on the same level of existence (and hence reliving lessons over again); or gains personal enlightenment, thus moving that specific 'life entity' to the next higher level of existence.

Additionally, numerous more modern and notable people have also embraced the concept of reincarnation, including Ralph Waldo Emerson, Walt Whitman, Jack London, Thomas Edison, William Blake, Sir Arthur Conan Doyle, Henry Miller, Gustav Mahler, Leo Tolstoy, General George Patton, and Henry Ford. Mr. Ford reportedly adopted his belief in reincarnation when he was 26 years of age, apparently questioning the rational: "What are we here for?"[24]

Mr. Ford believed such a question required real answers in order to give true meaning and purpose to life, otherwise life was empty and useless. He believed in a universal plan where time was not a limiting factor. It has been reported that NASA astronaut Ed Mitchell, although not publicly professing a firm belief in reincarnation, revealed that upon his approach for landing on the moon, felt a sudden awareness of having made the trip before.[25]

No proof is offered that reincarnation exists, since none is known. The same is true with all other beliefs associated with the cessation of corporeal life. Nor does this author have any intent to refute other ideologies in favor of reincarnation. Any religious concept, including the belief in reincarnation, is one that can not be proven solely with logic or scientific findings. Science has failed to adequately explain the bulk of enigmatic, occult, and paraphysical occurrences or events that apparently occasionally happen; yet the lack of explanation does not prevent such strange phenomenon from occurring.

The tenets of most world religions originally seemed to encompass personal reincarnation, so perhaps some connection might still remain, with the reincarnation creed 'quietly' continuing to underlie most religious dogma. Any true reincarnation belief welcomes such skepticism and scrutiny. Any thought, concept, hypothesis, or religious belief that is truly valid should always be able to withstand careful examination.

This writing suggests the existence of reincarnation, without actually offering it as a testable hypothesis, but rather as an intuitive belief (or perhaps as subconsciously retained knowledge). After exploring philosophical theories of more learned persons than myself, coupled with my present knowledge and human perspective, it is this writer's belief that humankind is incapable of truly understanding the mechanics and concepts that pertain to the realm beyond our material world. Such an intangible realm does not offer a discernible frame of reference from which physical comprehension could occur. Simply stated, while humanity is confined within the material world, we are incapable of grasping the true concept of an intangible domain. Such comprehension simply lacks any physical reference from which understanding might begin.

This writing is intended to expose only the most fundamental and basic elements within the reincarnation belief system. Since it is only natural to fear anything not fully understood, as well as harbor some doubts over those mysteries, certain preconceptions and confusion (perhaps from 'prior' incorrect teachings) might still exist. The following two chapters endeavor to explain individual elements within this belief system from my perspective, in order to establish a common understanding and clarification of the reincarnation concept. The subsequent remaining chapters in Part Two will then deal with how this belief system may affect and apply to 'every day' mortal life.

Chapter Four

Understanding

Although most people have heard of reincarnation, few have likely considered its concept without certain preconceived notions or feelings of anxiety. One tends to avoid or dismiss that which eludes comprehension, and therefore its ultimate understanding, especially if the subject may relate to an unconventional position or belief. Life apparently possesses many dimensions, some seen and others unseen. One can not physically see electricity or touch electromagnetic radiation such as radio waves, television broadcasts, microwaves, radar impulses, Gamma and X-rays, or any number of other similar phenomena; yet their existence is not questioned.

Humankind's physical tenure comprises birth, life, and death. Such commodities are also acknowledged without doubt, although sometimes without overwhelming embrace. They are simply known and accepted occurrences. The purpose and meaning of our mortal existence, as well as what transpires after our present cycle of life has ended, is the unknown part. That after-life explanation has been the subject of much debate, controversy, fear, conjecture, and doubt since humanity first developed an ability to contemplate abstract concepts.

Yet merely espousing a belief does not create factual reality. One needs and deserves some tangible substantiation or proof. While this writing does not present undeniable or reproducible evidence that reincarnation exists, neither does it disprove nor dispute any known facts. Rather, it offers an encompassing explanation for both the seen and unseen. It evaluates both the known aspects of physical life, as well as any unknown realm beyond corporeal existence.

In order to establish a comprehensive level to objectively evaluate the reincarnation concept, it is necessary to achieve commonalty with the terms and semantics associated with such a belief. The ensuing definitions and clarifications are intended to serve as a uniform starting point from which to further evaluate this concept.

Philosophy

Reincarnation is a philosophy of life that explains the purpose of physical existence and our spiritual immortality. It is the long-term journey of continual discovery and the perfection of each individual entity; a journey that simply can not be accomplished within only one span of physical life. Such an extensive and continuing journey can ultimately only be completed after the perfection of each individual essence is finally achieved, accompanied by a return back to its source, the Creator. It is the grand purpose of life, death, and rebirth; the repetitive cycle of physical existence. It involves the return of one's essence, that unique commodity that differentiates each of us as individuals from all others, to some ephemeral realm for further reflection, rejuvenation, and planning. Such an immortal essence may be referred to as our consciousness, mind, spirit, or soul; all different but generally interchangeable physical terms that apparently refer to the same commodity. This concept is recognized as Earth's oldest original spiritual belief, one revealed to early humans as part of what is now known as the *Ancient Wisdom.*

Reincarnation follows the inherent and intended perpetual order of nature, which displays changing seasons marked by the blossoming, nurturing, and subsequent contributions from each essence; growth that occurs over lengthy periods involving numerous continuing incarnations. It is like-becoming-like, with humans remaining human, and animals remaining animal; although some believe that 'lower animals' continue their subsequent evolution toward ever-higher forms of animals, eventually becoming 'entry-level' humans within such an ongoing process.

Process

Each life cycle is a continuing successive next step or stage within the ultimate learning and growth process of each individual, which is fundamental for any progress in obtaining personal 'character' perfection. Such an endeavor always requires positive contributions to the world in which each individual inhabits, while learning from 'object lessons' that are encountered throughout each incarnated life. Those encounters provide many opportunities or trials from which to shape each individual's innate character, through a learning process those life-lessons provide, allowing subsequent correction of retained faults that eventually lead to perfected traits. Such an ongoing process can eventually establish permanent intrinsic core values, which are achieved through small incremental steps that lead towards one's ultimate goal of perfection.

Interaction with humans and animals is always necessary for such a soul expansion process. An introvert may have less opportunity to learn from fewer encounters than an extrovert, but might more readily comprehend their intended meaning while achieving greater benefit from fewer encountered lessons throughout life. Likewise, an extrovert could have vastly more opportunities for correction and growth, as a result of increased exposure to potential learning events, and thus might achieve accelerated progress and enlightenment from merely a portion of the lessons they actually experience. An individual's pace of development is established solely by a willingness to identify their own short falls and deficiencies, when also accompanied with the required effort necessary to correct them.

One's perspective is equally important in dealing with

life's many trials or lessons. One's approach to adversity can be either a great help or a significant hindrance, depending on their outlook. Everyone should endeavor to always remain receptive, open, and objective in order to fully comprehend and benefit from every life experience that is constantly developing. One might entirely overlook or miss the intent of a specific lesson in life, if that person remains unreceptive. An open mind permits evaluation of all that life offers, allowing for measured responses to such events. Hence, numerous 'pluses' and 'minuses' are always associated with the many learning events that constantly surround all of us. One's free will offers many choices in responding to such events throughout life, but free will choice always comes with a price or reward. We are always responsible for our own actions. Essentially, what we sow, we also reap.

Although interaction is always a necessary ingredient for personal growth, care must be constantly exercised throughout all encounters made during life. Certain associations may have negative implications, thus impeding an individual's ultimate growth process. One reflects the actions of, and is known by the friends and associates they keep. One's choices must be wise, so as not to hinder their individual growth process. Peer pressure can often be the most damaging element preventing such personal growth. But free will choice offers discernment, the freedom not to associate with another individual, or partake in certain situations for whatever reason, as long as no anger or judgment is directed toward the encountered situation or person involved.

Nothing is permanent within the physical realm, which can be verified by observations made throughout nature. Change is always constant, no matter how slow or indiscernible it might seem. In humankind, the greatest and only lasting or truly eternal change comes from personal growth and enlightenment. Such change is brought about by expansion of one's consciousness or soul, through recognition of their own remaining personal character deficiencies, ones that are behavioral rather than physical deficiencies. That realization, when accompanied with a concentrated effort to modify those inadequacies, can then be channeled to obtain additional individual growth through correction of those retained faults. Such change can only come from within each unique individual, even though a catalyst from multiple outside influences, sources, or events might first initiate it as a result of one's life-path trials or lessons.

The lessons and tests that are encountered throughout life are always sufficient to provide the learning and growth that is necessary to implement those changes that are required within each developing entity. Regardless if the lesson is perceived as good or bad, it still exists. They will occur at certain planned times during life, for a specific learning purpose. Often one's initial perception is later altered or rethought as the wisdom resulting from those object lessons is ultimately understood and accepted, when also accompanied by its subsequent change over time. By maintaining control within our life, the required discipline necessary to achieve the serenity and understanding to initiate such transitions will naturally occur. However, we can only change ourselves. Conversely, we do not possess the ability or the right to attempt change in others.

Such learning never ceases, with continuing trials and lessons constantly encountered, which could result in further personal correction. Each future improvement adds to one's previous base, always building upon past gains within this personal corrective process. Physical death is also a necessary element for continued development and growth. It is a process of graduating from one 'grade' to the next higher level within this perpetual learning process. Inevitable death followed by subsequent rebirth provides the vital rejuvenation that is always necessary to cope with those specific additional trials that might require more physical stamina, thereby allowing for more challenging encounters that may be necessary for adequate resolution of long-retained faults.

Concept

The reincarnation process acknowledges the existence of one's soul, spirit, or consciousness; that nebulous commodity associated with every physical existence. This personal, immortal, but intangible commodity is what makes each of us 'ourselves,' unique and separate from all others, forming the very nature and basis of our identity. It is the imperceptible element that comprises one's essence, which goes beyond corporeal existence. While such a commodity has no material or tangible reality, it imparts the life force energy and physical awareness within its presently inhabited corporeal body, directing or determining its ultimate behavior. It is an ethereal commodity that can not die, generating life from a never-ending force. Such an essence transcends time itself, acting as a permanent foundation upon which we may continually build.

The soul evidently energizes and animates each physical body, the vessel that temporarily holds or 'houses' this ethereal essence, which is not a physical commodity, but a discarnate one. This consciousness or soul is evidently the source of thought, ideas, and reasoning, which are attributes we generally perceive as being associated with the physical brain or mind. It is the cohesive force that links one's physical and spiritual components, our core essence and current body, beyond a mere biological connection. It fuses, at least temporarily, those dissimilar elements in some sort of metaphysical manner. Each soul appears to be an intangible cosmic energy or force that can not be destroyed, but merely altered or reshaped as necessary for its continued learning and growth process, ultimately leading to the perfection of each core essence.

Arguably, each soul is unique and apparently a different commodity than the physical mind, which does not readily retain memories of prior incarnations associated with each individual essence. While the mind is apparently a function of the brain, a physical organ, the soul is ethereal and evidently the seat of each individual's moral values and character composition; that nebulous center from which intuition or 'gut-feelings' emerge to influence or direct our actions. Although the mind appears dependent on the physical existence of its body, the soul is apparently separate and immortal. It becomes 'complete' only within the ethereal realm where it is once again reunited with all past life experiences. Further, each soul is apparently a dual-commodity component. Perhaps the earliest ancient Egyptians best defined such a commodity. They differentiated between the *Ka* and *Ba*, distinct elements that supposedly comprised each soul, while forming a partial symbiotic relationship with one's physical existence. Although every physical body eventually perishes, a part of each soul, its *Ka*, then departs that deceased vessel (body) to rejoin with its cumulative and eternal counterpart, its *Ba* (also *Bai*), within the ethereal realm.[1] That spiritual joining then 'completes' each entity, reflecting their current level of development. It is from this combined status of our two soul components that we are temporarily reunited with all 'past experiences' while in the spiritual realm; 'completing' our essence with all its flaws, as well as every past accomplishment.

While all of our past existences stay with our *Ba* within the spiritual realm, there appears to be an unseen and unknown 'partial link' with that ethereal commodity while we are still in the physical world. It is only the presently developed 'core being' or current essence of one's self, both good and bad, that imprints upon our present *Ka* when it subsequently infuses with its new vessel at birth. Although the *Ba* within the spiritual realm retains all our past memories, 'major' or transformational events from prior lives may occasionally resurface during one's current life as a transitory glimpse or 'bits of information' from past existences. Therefore, perhaps some 'limited unification' or link might somehow exist between the spiritual and physical realms, temporarily connecting that *Ka* with its *Ba*.

It is merely our currently 'accumulated' essence or core composition that imprints with our present *Ka*. That essence is the sum total of what all our prior lives have produced (excluding past memories), combining all our 'perfected accomplishments' as well as our still-retained faults. It is that accumulated total that then represents the current evolution of our being; our character composition as a distinct individual, based on our present developmental level resulting from all our prior choices.

At the initial origin of each entity, every soul started out neutral, as if in a void, all equal-distance from both Good and Evil. No entity ever began its very first existence with any negative or positive behavioral characteristics. Every initial soul merely became a candidate for shaping, towards either Good or Evil, depending on which path each individual chose for their personal development. It is further speculated that not all souls were created at the time of the Big Bang event, with some planned to emerge as 'later creations,' as future worlds eventually formed from the expansion of our universe.

Each consciousness must overcome essentially the same set of trials and lessons, or similar 'test' requirements, to achieve eventual perfection. Every entity's life-experiences and lessons are essentially common, with their occurrence during some incarnation when those lessons are most appropriate. While such trials and lessons may be slightly different in severity, substance, or frequency, depending on each individual's need or acceptance to learn from those encounters; every consciousness must ultimately confront, endure, and overcome essentially equivalent obstacles at some planned time during successive lives. One's collection of acquired innate traits and character composition, either negative or positive, then eventually accumulate to determine one's individual perfection of either Good or Evil.

The elemental being of one's existence, our essence, soul, or consciousness, is what bonds with and animates our physical vessel, which is then used to experience mortal life. That bond is broken at death, releasing each consciousness back to the spiritual realm for further introspection and evaluation, prior to rebonding with a subsequent vessel within the physical world. Perhaps the spiritual realm is the elementary dimension, with one's soul or consciousness relegated to the size and laws associated with the quantum level. If so, the essence of each soul would likely occupy merely a single point within a two-dimensional spiritual realm, where the order and harmony of space-time would not apply. Such an existence may lack predictability, with all events occurring simultaneously in a state of 'ordered' chaos, one without a perceived beginning or end. Such a condition would allow events to be predestined, while one's different interactions with those events would be determined by individual free will choice, allowing an infinite number of outcomes from each destined event. That spiritual realm of pure energy, or universal consciousness, might also be the central point from which all 'thought' emanates.

The soul is universal, able to possess any physical vessel on any planet within our universe. It is not limited by, or dependent upon, any specific species or environment. Any suitable physical vessel or body could accommodate such an ethereal commodity for its subsequent incarnations. The ultimate selection of a specific world, and hence a subsequent compatible species for reincarnation, would be determined by the future destined events associated with each individual conjunction. One can learn from any environment or setting, regardless which planet those lessons might ultimately transpire upon. The truly important consideration involves our 'lesson events' that are destined to occur, regardless of their time frame or location in which those lessons actually transpire, or even the type of species that will eventually

49

encounter those destined events.

A conscious self-awareness of each 'soul entity' apparently exists in both the spiritual and material worlds. It is constant in its reality, whether inhabiting a corporeal body in the mortal world, or when in true spirit-form while on the 'other side.' It is both objective and subjective at once. What is perceived as 'individual reality' by one's mind within the physical world can apparently transcend death and continue to function non-stop within the spiritual realm beyond, while continuing its cycle of continuity through its later return for a successive new mortal life. There is never an interruption of any consciousness, merely a suppression of past memory upon return to the mortal world, for habitation within another 'new' corporeal body.

As previously stated, the ancient predynastic Egyptians knew that the body was mortal, believing the present soul, which they knew as the *Ka*, ultimately transcended physical death, at least temporarily. The *Ka* or soul may even be an individual part of the universal spirit or 'component' of the Creator that enters each body at birth, which also provides immortality for each essence or consciousness. Those earliest Egyptians also knew that the current soul was not the total constituent or component of any individual's consciousness or essence. They were aware of an additional element, the *Ba*, which was the soul's nebulous 'companion commodity' that always remained within the ethereal realm, separate from its *Ka*, during each subsequent *Ka*'s occupation of a new physical body during successive physical incarnations.

The release of the soul after physical death allowed both the *Ka* and *Ba* to once again be reunited within the ethereal or spiritual realm, thus 'completing' each consciousness, at least temporarily. Each released *Ka* brings its most recent life's events, lessons, corrections, failures, and newly gained knowledge back to the previously accumulated 'whole' of that individual essence, its *Ba*. Such an interim 'combination' or reuniting of the *Ka* and *Ba* then reflects the current progress or evolution of that individual essence, representing that entity's complete awareness and obtained level of knowledge; restoring all past components, elements, and memories of its distinct composition. That temporary 'unified completeness' then reflects one's present progress toward ultimate perfection that has been obtained so far by that individual.

The Egyptian god Thoth confirmed this dual nature of the soul. He reported that only one fragment of our spirit or soul, the *Ka*, actually entered the physical body, while the other part, its *Ba*, remained behind within the 'timeless' spiritual realm.[2] Similar beliefs arose independently throughout many parts of the ancient world, with this concept becoming an integral part of the early collection of knowledge commonly known as the *Ancient Wisdom*. Such knowledge revealed reincarnation to be the process that provides immortality for each life, while also revealing the imperishability of the eternal soul.

The Hindus and Gnostics, along with an array of early philosophers, including Pythagoras, Origen, Clement of Alexanderia, and Socrates, all believed in the duality of the soul. Each theorized that the Creator had infused into every physical entity a portion of the Creator's Divine Spirit, which animated life. They concluded that humans possessed two souls that were of separate and different natures. One was the *Astral Soul* that infused with the entire physical body (same as the *Ka*). That soul is 'perishable,' meaning it ends when its current vessel (body) ceases animation (dies). Upon physical death, this element would then fuse with the *Augoeide*, the incorruptible and immortal portion of the Divine Spirit (the 'ethereal' soul, same as the *Ba*) that remained within the spiritual realm.[3] Each 'fusion' of these two 'soul components' was intended to produce a more 'purified' entity at the conclusion of each transmigration (reincarnated physical life). The ultimate conclusion to this ongoing process would be the reabsorption of a 'perfected' soul back into the Creator.[4]

The *Ka* is said to inhabit the entire form of the body it

animates, becoming an image or 'double' of that vessel. Perhaps this concept helps to explain the 'ghost image' of certain deceased persons that are occasionally reported. Such sightings are usually very brief encounters and may reflect a 'confused' *Ka* that is simply unaware of the physical death of its vessel and its subsequent release or separation from its now-dead body. Such an image of the 'deceased' may linger until it finally 'crosses-over' to the spiritual realm for reunification with its *Ba*. One may speculate that such an entity's reincarnation process is temporarily interrupted until its *Ka* and *Ba* fully integrates within the ethereal domain.

Physical Body

One's temporal body is used to experience physical events for growth and expansion of its consciousness. While such growth can occur within the spiritual realm, it is in the material world where the greatest opportunity for progress is offered, due to physical temptations and interactions. Since every consciousness is at a different level of understanding within its own growth process, so every physical person is also at different stages of character development. That accounts for the vast disparity among humankind. Each individual mortal life is used as a classroom in which to learn and hopefully improve one's level of understanding, thus allowing corrections of faults while providing an increase in spiritual enlightenment. Conversely, failure to learn from such life-lessons assures personal stagnation without growth, and perhaps a path toward Evil, if such lessons are consistently avoided and necessary corrections are not made.

Each body or vessel is a gift on loan from the Creator. It requires respect, protection, and care to assure that its physical ability is not compromised, thereby permitting achievement of one's current tasks. Each body also demands that its intended life-span duration be fulfilled, allowing all of one's 'planned lessons and trials' to be presented. Bodily death merely provides a necessary regenerative process, while also allowing time for reflection and assessment. Physical death sustains the mechanism for those incremental 'stepping stones' along one's continuing path of existence. The 'physical realm' is merely condensed energy, arranged in a certain pattern at an intended density, within its uniquely specific time frame. When released from the confines of physical laws, that same energy still exists, but as a 'free-state' of pure energy within the spiritual realm. The mind, body, and spirit are all aspects of the same commodity, and undergo 'conversions' similar to changes encountered with each new corporeal vessel upon subsequent incarnations.

According to teachings of the Egyptian god Thoth, future incarnations might involve a different race, gender, or perhaps even species (such as an existence or life on another planet) based on each essence's evolutionary needs. All such selections are dependent on an individual's level of enlightenment, and their recognition and desire to address deficiencies that still remain, all within the limitation of choices such an entity has 'earned' through their past efforts and accomplishments toward perfection of their character composition.

Physical Death

When our temporal body dies, our consciousness is once again released to the spiritual side. Such a release provides for a review of what has been learned and accomplished, as well as a critique of mistakes made during one's latest tangible life experience. One's consciousness is once again expanded to its greater or 'total' awareness and understanding, reflective of one's true 'enlightenment level,' unencumbered by limitations of the recently 'discarded' physical senses. This state reflects the temporary reunification of one's *Ka* and *Ba*. Remembrance of all past existences, previous relationships and events, and one's 'purpose lessons' planned for the most recently completed material life then readily return to that consciousness in their entirety.

After introspection and self-judgment of one's most recent physical existence, the next mortal life is planned, choosing a path containing future learning experiences that are necessary for further growth. Somewhat later, one's consciousness or soul once again enters or merges with another new physical body, in the form of a baby at the time of its physical birth.

There is limited evidence that the spiritual essence of an individual may even spend time with its intended parents-to-be while still in spirit form, 'hovering' around to better know them, in an effort to become sufficiently acquainted with their future surroundings, environment, and parental influences. Upon birth, one's 'classroom' of learning experiences once again begins, allowing life's current lessons to unfold, providing events from which character traits can be formed. This process is repeated over and over, all with the goal of obtaining the highest or ultimate divine level of perfection, one of total acceptance and knowledge.

As a newborn infant, we enter this world with a far greater level of understanding than is generally ascribed by science. That comprehension includes limited temporary knowledge of certain aspects of prior lives, along with an innate awareness of the reincarnation process. But due to our helpless and vulnerable status, our focus is on food, care, and survival. When babies dream, they may recall glimpses of major events from their past lives. As they grow, very young children are often aware of certain knowledge that had never been exposed to them during their present short existence. Certain prior transformational events can become so deeply ingrained that they imprint upon our essence and are retained as nebulous fleeting memories from another past. Theses misty flashes, vague dreams, and wispy glimpses dissipate and fade as we grow older, as our mind becomes more focused on all the stimuli within the present, not the past.

Most of these prior life connections will normally fully disappear by roughly the age of seven years old.

Still, such recollections of prior existences are apparently limited at any age, similar to a computer being constrained by its memory storage capacity. The human mind or consciousness, as well as our subconscious, simply does not seem adequate to retain all past life memories while in the physical realm. This apparent limitation seems to restrict the amount of information that can actually be obtained through regressive hypnosis, *déjà vu* experiences, channeling/séance sessions, dream therapy, or other similar techniques. But it is of lesser significance who we were previously, since the past can not be changed. Rather, the importance lies with what we can become in the future, based on what we do presently.

Immortality

Reincarnation was the process most ancient religions cited for humanity's spiritual immortality. Over time, due to both secular and religious influences, the reincarnation doctrine became distorted or suppressed. Although starting during ancient times, it stalled with the emergence of Dynastic Egypt. But it once again became prominent after the sixth century BC, continuing into our current era when the prior concept of a nondescript afterlife, known as Sheol, was replaced with either a belief in a heavenly paradise, or a demonic inferno. Such a 'one-shot' existence then allowed redemption at the 'eleventh hour,' even after a disgraceful life, by ultimately embracing a specific deity and requesting forgiveness. However, another individual that might have led a neutral or uneventful life but never worshipped such an 'acceptable' deity would be refused similar salvation. It is only reasonable to expect a more equitable spiritual system with greater universal fairness.

Such fairness appears to be the commodity known in ancient times as *karma*. Karma, which means 'action,' is the natural or universal law connected with every event encountered in life. It can not be fooled or deceived. Mere remorse and guilt can not cancel karma; it requires repair, repentance, and action leading to atonement in the form of future good deeds, in order to offset any deficiencies caused by prior transgressions. Karma is not a teaching tool or a punishment; it is a debt or imbalance that must be offset through future actions as repayment. Infliction of injury is always corrected through similar justice, while kindness is repaid in kind. Many have interpreted Jesus' statement, "...as ye sow, so shall ye reap," as alluding to karma. Karma will be discussed further in the section dealing with 'prices,' presented later in this chapter.

Free Will

The Oriental idea of reincarnation involves birth into the physical world at a chosen time, precisely at one's place of birth from specifically chosen parents; all entwined with the particular destiny that distinct life would provide. Simply put, such a birth scenario was what the individual chose, needed, and required for their own ultimate illumination. However, dynastic Egyptians and the later Classic Greeks both believed that human destiny or fate was decided before birth, with no power to alter its ultimate direction. Hence, they thought that human destiny was an immutable commodity.

Such a belief is a distortion or misconception of free will choice within the larger context of encountered 'predestined' events. While a future event may be predestined to occur sometime during a specifically chosen life, one's free will choice in reacting to those fated learning events will determine their ultimate lasting effect. Such an event may be completely ignored, discounting its lesson and discarding its intended opportunity for any character development. The ultimate choice always remains with each individual.

Lessons

One's positive purpose during each physical existence is to grow spiritually through correction of retained negative behavioral traits, by learning 'lessons' from life's experiences. That requires one to be receptive to all surrounding events, while keeping an open mind without prejudice or preconceived ideas. Many of life's lessons involve more perplexing aspects of existence, since we learn from the difficult, not the easy events. One will repeat mistakes over and over until their lessons are learned. As a result of this corrective process, we can eventually add to our permanent 'core' or basic character-composition. Only then can one's positive intuitive responses and actions toward future occurrences become automatic and innate in their implementation.

The quantity and degree of trials for each present life are set before birth, as one's lessons to learn. Those lessons are always based upon our current capacity and ability (or enlightenment level) to learn. *No lesson ever encountered in any life is beyond one's present comprehension or capability.* One's behavioral deficiencies are fully recognized and understood subconsciously, and manifest within the trials and lessons that are encountered throughout each successive life's learning experiences. Any progress requires us to confront and overcome those retained faults.

Every life provides unique challenges or trials based on the societal time frame during which each life-path occurs. Less developed times can provide physical hardships that more modern settings might not. However, our contemporary societies may offer current conveniences that can provide different types of demands and tests. The noticeable moral declines that have occurred within our modern 'progressive' culture create numerous impediments to those seeking higher spiritual pursuits. Overcrowding on our planet, with its continually increasing population level, may also produce more irritations and direct conflicts with other inhabitants. The numerous complexities associated with modern life certainly contribute to the frustrations and impatience we encounter in everyday life. The proliferation of ever more devastating weapons can spread greater fear and insecurity throughout most global populations. The compression of more duties and demands on our limited time adds to those frustrations. The accumulation of money, along with pursuit of pleasure and material possessions, can further cloud one's judgments, values, and priorities. Envy of those perceived to be more accomplished, happier, richer, or more attractive, also compounds individual insecurities and frustrations.

One may not recognize life's lessons, but they are always present throughout mortal life. Recognition is the initial step for deficiency correction within this ongoing learning process. Understanding such character deficiencies as counter-productive towards life's purpose is the second phase. Subsequent modification or adjustment in our attitude or perspective, which may be contributing to negative behavioral reactions toward life's events or relationships, becomes the next level within this corrective process. Implementation of positive and permanent intuitive character changes (one's conditioned responses), which can be achieved through introspective wisdom and a true desire for change, is the final stage in mastering any deficiency or fault. An active and conscious effort must be deliberately undertaken, accepting responsibility for all necessary changes, if one is to permanently overcome and replace their present deviant behavioral traits.

It must be stressed that one's life-path or destiny, the plan from which intended life-lessons emerge and are experienced, is set before birth. However, our free will choice allows an infinite number of options, and hence different outcomes, for every encountered incident in life. Events that offer learning experiences are neither random, nor occur by chance. Rather, those events simply manifest or emerge within our lives at specific times when we are fully able to deal with their intended lessons or trials.

This can be a very difficult concept to comprehend. Humankind has a tendency to view life as either a predestined event with no individual choice; or as a totally random occurrence, but with complete control exercised by all individuals. Rather, it appears that a combination of these two seemingly opposing convictions constitute our true reality; along with a realization that we are ultimately in control of every action, even though certain encounters or destined events will take place sometime within our presently-planned life. Such events could, but not necessarily will, have a profound affect upon our life. They merely offer an opportunity for such a consequential impact. That tends to indicate the existence of a dualism concept, combining the seemingly opposing beliefs of indeterminism and fatalism. While being distinct and different concepts, they are not necessarily opposing beliefs, and may actually complement one another. Although dissimilar, they are fully compatible within both their composition and ultimate effect.

It is accepted that future locations of celestial bodies can be determined by calculating and plotting their orbital course. The same is true for climatic jet stream paths and pressure fronts. As an example, consider a simple weather forecast. Rain is expected, occurring sometime in the near future. But our individual responses to such a destined event are limitless, with each different response possibly shaping or altering our fundamental being, depending upon which course of action is pursued. Consider a planned community picnic that falls on the day of that forecasted rain. Because of the rain, one may choose not to go, thus avoiding being hit by lightening that strikes, injuring those in attendance. Or another may choose to attend and be introduced to the love of their life, leading to marriage. The predestined event, the rain, is going to happen. One's own free will choice allows numerous responses to such a set occurrence.

Variations of outcomes from one's choices are infinite. Such free will action may produce a profound result in one's present life, either as a positive change, such as marriage; or result in a disabling injury, resulting from a lightening strike. Or perhaps the intended 'trial' will simply manifest once again later in life, when a similar occurrence may be appropriate; or one may manage to entirely forestall such ominous situations, completely avoiding possible injury. Choices always exist, with one's life-path events seldom posing an 'either-or' scenario, without ample available alternatives.

Life's pre-planned episodes are more involved than merely predicting rain during some future event. The intricacies of such life-path occurrences may compound as one becomes involved within their development, with each step leading to still another destined occurrence. Still, no outcome is ever preset or fixed. No final fate is determined until one individually chooses the extent of their involvement with each event. Results of future history have not yet been established as fact, merely the impending historical event is destined, with an infinite number of different outcomes.

Consider the intriguing life and 'visions' of Michael de Nostradamus (1503-1566 AD), the noted French physician, astronomer, scientist, and prognosticator. His visions of the future are among the most renowned and studied over the ages. Nostradamus made over 1,000 predictions of impending events. His prophecies were based on ten future centuries, grouped in sets of ten, written in rhyming quatrains. Some of Nostradamus' most notably accurate predictions include:

1. The foretold emergence of a simple friar named Felice Peretti, who would become Pope Sixtus V in 1585.
2. The occurrence of the French Revolution in 1791, along with specific details including a remarkably accurate accounting of actual events. Those future visions reported highly detailed personal accounts

60

involving both King Louis XVI and Marie
Antoinette.
3. An extensive description of the reign, conquests, and
   ultimate dual defeats of Napoleon.
4. The accurate descriptive details of Germany's rise to
   power, apparently under Hitler, and the events of
   World War II.
5. Details of the events and the emergence of an
   Arabian warlord during the 1990s, who would
   ultimately threaten world peace and precipitate
   World War III.

It is important to note that Nostradamus himself strongly
believed that humanity could master fate, and that the future
could be changed. Perhaps certain major occurrences that
Nostradamus did not foretell may have been added to
humankind's future 'schedule-of-events,' due to the
deterioration of civilization since his time. Likewise, certain
developments that were foreseen by Nostradamus but did not
transpire might have later been deemed 'unnecessary' due to
social 'corrections' implemented by humanity, thereby
negating such required future envisioned events.

The original Persian Gulf War with Iraq, which emanated
from the invasion of Kuwait in 1990, has often been cited as
the prediction that Nostradamus foretold as occurring during
the 1990s with an Arabian warlord ruler, one similar to
Saddam Hussein. If the actions that occurred before the
ensuing 1991 United Nations Desert Storm War were the
events that Nostradamus had foreseen during the sixteenth
century, our future history might have indeed been altered by
later humankind's subsequent actions. However, that event
may have merely been a prequel to some future occurrence.
Perhaps present Near East tensions and various related
terrorists groups may have replaced a single entity with a
larger movement. Or possibly Nostradamus' prediction was
merely postponed to some later time during our twenty-first

century. The subsequent war in Iraq launched after September 11, 2001 may be part of such a 'replacement event' associated with that original prediction. Perhaps we may never know, or merely not meant to know the true nature of such complex rationalizations, interactions, and schemes that are associated with future events.

Although this author possesses a neutral opinion as to any 'claimed ability' to foretell the future, or the factual validity of psychics, mystic seers, or those in other similar vocations; evidence of rare but gifted individuals similar to Nostradamus occasionally surface. Such fated 'visionaries' seem to appear at various intervals throughout history. More modern examples include two such gifted or endowed individuals, namely Edgar Cayce (1877-1945) and Eileen Garrett (1893-1970). Both demonstrated powers beyond normally understood levels, and withstood refute of their abilities from the scientific community numerous times. Their impact on the future, as to how life itself might unfold and develop, can not yet be fully evaluated.

Yet their influence on humanity's interaction with future unfolding events, from a potential response to merely one of their predictions, might create a domino effect that essentially changes the course of future human history. Such visions may shape an entirely different direction from the one that was originally intended, without ever knowing what might have been previously planned. The nature, purpose, intent, and reason for such 'gifted exceptions' are most likely not meant to be explained or understood by the general populace, at least not as of this writing.

Prophesy may not be the ability to actually 'see' into the future, but rather a capacity to deduce the most logical probabilities from established and known parameters that underlie each situation. A statistical evaluation of every likely outcome, balanced with all their possible but identifiable repercussions and consequences, might allow a determination of which scenario is most likely to occur as a result of any potentially implemented action. Such critical review of all potential outcomes from multiple circumstances or scenarios might then predict the most likely result that would be associated with those future occurrences. Thus, as all effects from our current actions are projected into the future, the contours of such 'future events' might have ultimately been set in motion, or commenced their eventual development during present times.

Purpose

One's present life-path, a commodity incorrectly interpreted as possessing an unchangeable outcome, is preset before birth. Its multitude of predestined events, trials, relationships, and encounters, those episodes through which one will traverse life, ultimately provide lessons from which learning and correction can occur. But one must allow life's events to develop and unfold. Too often we simply forestall those destined events by trying too hard, or by postponing and avoiding life. Live life through active participation, becoming a part of its web of entanglement, without fear of 'taking chances' or attempting that 'first step.' One's free will allows a limitless choice of actions and responses to those life-path experiences, thereby ultimately controlling and determining their resultant outcomes. Thus, we are always in control of our own fate.

The very concept of a Higher Power, one possessing the necessary intelligence to have planned the Big Bang event, implies that a specific purpose was involved in the creation of physical life. Conversely, an underlying goal or purpose within physical life would seem to imply the existence of a Supreme Being. Perhaps a more correctly stated perspective simply implies that without intelligence, purpose can not exist. Deciding which came first, the product or the concept, merely creates a circular argument, one in which the conclusion also appears as an assumption within its logical argument. Perhaps the underlying purpose of creation is so complex that its design intent presently remains beyond human comprehension.

It would also seem logical that any imparted knowledge would come with the intention for its sensible use, leading to some productive result or outcome. Thus, physical life apparently requires practical actions, in the form of worthwhile deeds or work-related accomplishments to fulfill some primary purpose. These individual contributions from personal productivity should logically involve certain carry-over traits or affinities previously mastered, ones associated with certain skills, vocational abilities, talents, or interests. Such 'prior' inclinations or aptitudes would seemingly entice one to gravitate toward certain disciplines or studies. Those retained attributes would have likely been cultivated during past lives, although they may be inhibited or perhaps limited by certain circumstances associated with one's present or 'new-life' environment.

Life experiences are part of the learning process that leads to correction, growth, and greater enlightenment. Nothing happens in life by accident. There is always purpose within every life-event. Regardless if that purpose becomes clear or not, or if it unfolds now or in the future, all events contain real value. Something can always be learned from every life-path occurrence, regardless if good or bad, insignificant or great. The purpose of physical life is to learn from such encountered trials, always with the intent to improve one's innate character. Such purpose is ultimately accomplished by overcoming one's retained or existing behavioral deficiencies through personal correction, thereby achieving desired change and subsequent growth.

Such growth produces an expansion of enlightenment within each individual's character development. A positive attitude and an openness to change appear to be essential requirements for any progress toward such continued personal growth. Balance in every facet of life is fundamental in achieving this desired understanding and knowledge, allowing one to cope with those troubled times that are often encountered throughout life's journey.

Balance

There is always balance in nature. The physical body allows humankind to be out of harmony with the natural world due to temptations, character deficiencies, and retained faults. Personal perceptions of events affecting each individual may be further distorted by their physical senses. Those false perceptions then shield us from the true reality of what actually exists, and thus often produce incorrect conclusions. Acquisition of knowledge and its accompanying wisdom, which is obtained through incremental personal growth, imparts the discipline necessary to prevent the faulty reactions that can result from one's incorrect perceptions and premature conclusions.

Maintaining contact with reality permits practical responses to any encountered event, rather than merely reacting to those occurrences. One is either going toward their goal, or away from it, depending on their thoughts, attitudes, and actions toward all things encountered within the material world. Our free will always allows numerous choices when responding to life's events.

Throughout life we are motivated by a subconscious desire for ultimate understanding and acceptance, wherein we become one with the universe, in a state of complete harmony. But distractions arising from temptations can alter our course away from that aspiration, delaying any progress. The wrong way in life is easy, while the right way is usually more difficult. One may continually fight those inherent instincts that offer guidance during perplexing choices in life, but it is ultimately our responsibility to achieve that required correction and growth. Pessimism can cloud our judgment and deter that process, while optimism opens the mind and promotes growth. One's outlook becomes self-perpetuating, with pessimism continuing to breed further negatives, while optimism fosters positive beliefs. Either attitude is solely the choice of each individual.

Values

We tend to complicate life, but the basics are simply the universal truths of Good and Evil. One's individually nurtured and inherent core values, sometimes known as our 'conscience,' guide us in our responses to the perceived 'gray areas' of right-and-wrong that are encountered during life. In real terms, there are no 'gray areas,' only the Natural Law of absolute Good or Evil. Natural Law is a theoretically 'higher law,' a universal code or moral truth that is ever constant.

Such a law forms a fundamental element of human nature. Natural Law concludes that an individual's 'rights' end when their actions infringe on the rights of others. Such a concept is an altruistic attitude toward life, with respect for the interests of others always trumping any selfish motives. While extenuating circumstances are a consideration in secular or civil law, all actions are either positive or negative when gauged against their effects on the greater universe. Stealing is stealing, lying is lying, murder is murder, and so on. As we gain enlightenment, those 'gray areas' decrease and will eventually disappear completely from our perception.

While every initial soul started as a 'neutral' entity, originally equal distance from either Good or Evil, the result of experiencing just one mortal life starts the formulation of basic values within each 'candidate' soul. Such choices may produce basic positive values like compassion, honesty, duty, morality, and integrity; or the basic negative traits of hatred, greed, contempt, vulgarity, impulsiveness, intolerance, and deceit. Our parents, friends, religion, school, and admired role models often initially influence our choices toward one of those basic attributes. Those influences can frequently shape our initial responses toward many early life-path trials. It is only natural to possess both negative and positive traits during our early formative process. As an individual affinity toward either positive or negative traits is slowly established through free will choice, one then embarks toward their chosen path of Good or Evil. As that direction is chosen, one develops and reflects traits associated with such a life-path. However, individual free will choice is always available throughout life, allowing one to stay-the-course, or make conscious decisions to drastically change, thereby altering their initially chosen path.

Values are cumulative from life to life, and are retained by one's subconscious during each temporal existence. Such values allow for intuitive 'conditioned' responses reflecting one's present nature or true character toward current events encountered throughout each subsequent incarnation. They also form the foundation of our character makeup at the start of each new life, at whatever level of previously obtained enlightenment that had been achieved.

Hence, one's present 'being' reflects the true spiritual level that has been obtained through their character development over all previous lifetimes. It is that spiritual component that is raised or lowered in enlightenment, depending on how one responds to events experienced during their present physical life. Thus, one's current attitudes and actions towards life's events either add to their base character in a positive manner or undermine it. Or perhaps we choose to live a current life that merely allows us to remain stagnate at our previously attained level.

Such 'character values' may further be described as one's ethical or moral composition. Such attributes are also commonly used to define the rules for proper conduct or 'correct behavior.' They serve as a guide or reference as to how one might best conduct daily life in order to obtain positive results. Those guidelines need not be derived solely from religious beliefs. It must be recognized that people without a specific religious affiliation can also lead ethically moral lives, although such a life may require more effort, while perhaps also producing additional 'mistakes' within the process. Past and current lessons from our life-experiences, along with our inner-voice, conscience, or 'gut' feelings can also guide us in determining our behavioral responses.

Cosmic Record

Past lives provide the composition of each entity's core value system, within their present level of development. Some might refer to this 'component' as the previously mentioned inner-voice, gut feeling, or even one's conscience; that nebulous commodity providing each of us with an 'internal compass' that helps determine which actions may be either proper or erroneous. Such vague intuitions are shaped by lessons learned during our present and past lives, with all those events creating a permanent record shaping each individual's journey toward personal perfection.

Quantum physics claims that all events taking place throughout the universe leave marks on the subatomic level. Perhaps past-life events are recorded on that same level, one linked with the spiritual realm. If so, it would be logical that such a record could somehow be retrieved and reviewed. This concept may have been the inspiration for the belief in the Akashic Record, which ancient Sanskrit texts claim to be the permanent record of all prior actions that have left their mark on the cosmic level. The Akashic Record is described as a 'cosmic memory,' one that stores all actions and recollections of past events everywhere from within our physical universe, over all prior ages. It is believed by some that a truly enlightened consciousness might somehow be able to access that permanent cosmic record while still within the physical realm.

That concept parallels our present theory of peering into

deep space to view the Big Bang event, or at least its early results. By looking back 'far enough' in space, one theoretically could witness that event by viewing 'light' given off at the time of the Big Bang, which would still be detectable at its most remote point, as those early photons continue to travel at the speed of light.

However, similar past knowledge comprising the Akashic Record is commonly blocked from each individual during any subsequent corporeal existence, so as not to influence, overwhelm, or interfere with the learning process associated with their current life's lessons. Such past memory suppression is an absolute requirement. Otherwise we could force ourselves into positions or feelings we want to achieve, dominated by a subconscious knowledge of our present life-path lessons that are intended to overcome a specific deficiency. One must allow a natural inclination or tendency to develop, with a desire to truly embrace such a 'new' trait while abandoning its previously held opposite fault. Otherwise, that characteristic or attribute can not become innate and inherent. If such responses or traits are false or forced, one simply becomes deluded or compromised, with that encountered life-lesson ultimately resulting in failure.

Hidden Memory

It is further believed by some that an individual's present-life subconscious may also store certain important prior events as a 'selective' history of one's past lives. It is believed that such 'files' are highlights from the Akashic Record retained within the spiritual realm. If indeed one has lived before, it is perplexing that no conscious memory or even a portion of recollection exists of those past life experiences during our present existence. Consider the effects of medically diagnosed amnesia, and how it can fully suppress or block all recent memory of one's life. Hence, it is then certainly conceivable that a more powerful and subtle form of 'amnesia' may be invoked during our current life to repress any prior-life memories. Although we may not be able to readily recall events from a previous life, that does not exclude the possibility that such a past existence actually occurred. The Egyptian *Papyrus of Anana* apparently recognized such hidden prior memory, claiming: "Man comes into being many times, yet known nothing of his past lives...."[5]

The old adage, "Ignorance is Bliss," may apply in the case of reincarnation. If one were to realize the hardships and seeming unfairness of certain lessons, self-pity and personal resistance might overcome any incentive or desire to endure their present trial or test. Fortunately, it is often much later when an individual might actually realize the unfairness associated with such an earlier encountered specific trial. Some comfort can be derived from such belated realization, wherein that lesson's magnitude was not apparent at the time of its initial presentation, which might have discouraged any further participation with that challenging event.

Prior knowledge may also wrongly influence our reaction to present 'distasteful' encounters, or prejudice an individual toward many other future lessons. The best approach would be to focus on the ultimate goal of perfection as we deal with all trials that might be encountered during life, without becoming distracted or discouraged from pursuing our underlying purpose in life.

Additionally, humanity seems to resist change, a condition that appears to increase as one ages. If past memories were a confluent or continuous quantity from life to life with their conveyance into our current existence, all 'prior thoughts' would likely remain strongly held and defended. New technologies and contemporary thinking would then be firmly resisted, perhaps at the cost of negating any additional progress. That attitude can be detected from the resistance some elderly citizens have toward our latest innovations, such as electronic banking or personal computers and tablets, as they exhibit distrust with such new technology while preferring their 'old ways.' Likewise, prior thoughts and theories, including incorrect teachings and biases, would also be defended against any future 'corrected' findings, new hypotheses, or innovative ideas.

However, that same suppression of knowledge could also negate further progress, or at least its potentially quicker rate of achievement by not building upon or extending prior educational levels and past accomplishments into our next life-existence; with this process requiring that we 'start over' with the bare fundamentals. That argument breaks down with the understanding that all past knowledge is readily available to subsequent generations through each culture's written records and scientific documents. Such knowledge is thus accessible for future scrutiny and expansion.

A prior 'genius' in genetics would seemingly gravitate toward that field in a subsequent life, and would not only be able to perhaps build upon their own past 'documented' discoveries, but may also approach 'old' unsolved dilemmas with completely new approaches. Not only might new perspectives and procedures be introduced, but also a rejuvenated 'younger' level of energy could then be focused upon those efforts within that person's subsequent 'next life.'

Such acquired expertise and traits are developed subtly within the character composition of each entity, and serve as a tangible link with their prior experiences. Ignorance of reincarnation may even become a hindrance or deterrent in accomplishing current tasks during one's present life. Knowledge of the reincarnation process can be extremely beneficial and helpful in recognizing and obtaining the goals intended for correction during present life. Yet progress can always be achieved by doing the proper or right things, which parallels the precepts preached by most religious beliefs. However, one can ultimately fail when 'mere belief' within any individual doctrine is elevated above the required 'effort' necessary to achieve any actual correction and growth.

The mind apparently retains some continuation or

continuity with its previous life existence. Within normal life, glimpses of 'past flashbacks' and the inexplicable or overwhelming affinity towards specific events, objects, and other individuals may occur. Those occasional flashes or recognition of prior life interests are dismissed by our conscious mind, in an effort to maintain sanity and avoid any confusion. Meditation, regressive hypnosis, or dreams may release bits and pieces of those past life memories to our present-self while within the physical realm. However, such glimpses of one's past are generally dismissed as mere imaginings. The Egyptian *Papyrus of Anana* claimed that it is each person's *Ka* that can reveal these truthful glimpses of our past.[6]

Similar to values, one's anxieties, phobias, and other behavioral deficiencies are also carried over from past lives. That 'baggage' will remain a part of one's composition until they learn to overcome its fear. Nearly all negative responses, actions, and deviant behaviors have their basis deeply rooted in fear. It is through understanding that fear is ultimately defeated. Fear is one of two fundamental emotions forming the basis for human reaction, with the other being love. These two stimuli most often guide, influence, or motivate the majority of responses and actions within daily life. Those emotions help shape our behavioral development, while also influencing resultant thoughts, actions, and attitudes toward most encounters throughout life.

Suppressed Recollection

Perhaps no ancient culture understood the concept of repressed memory better than predynastic Egypt. Their notion of a dual component soul, the *Ka* and *Ba*, seems to best convey this concept. The *Ka* serves as the active conscious element during one's present existence, recording all events, mistakes, and accomplishments throughout our current life. Upon death, the *Ka* merges with its *Ba*, the ethereal element

72

of each soul that always remains within the spiritual realm. The *Ba* retains the complete earlier record comprising all past deeds of its individual entity, prior to its present incarnation. With the merging of both elements after death of the latest physical existence, the cumulative total record once again becomes 'whole' with the return of its *Ka*, which then includes that entity's most recent life. That combined *Ba* and *Ka* 'chronicle,' with all its accomplishments and past mistakes fully recorded, reveals the present status of that individual's progress, as well as any deficiencies still awaiting correction within their overall purpose or goal toward personal perfection. A new 'blank' *Ka* later integrates with a subsequently 'chosen' newborn baby to continue this ongoing building-block process within its next life.

Think of the *Ka* as a flash drive memory that is formatted with the core characteristics of its entity, but without specific memories of past life events that had shaped those values and traits. Those intrinsic values become our gut feelings that help to guide our free will choices. During present life, the *Ka* 'flash drive' records and stores our responses to all of our life-path events. Upon death, the *Ka* then reunites with its *Ba* in the spiritual realm. Think of the *Ba* as the main frame hard drive for each entity, containing all memories of past lives for that specific individual. The flash drive *Ka* is downloaded to the *Ba* main frame, adding all the events recorded during the most recent life. That unification then represents all the cumulative actions and current enlightenment level of that individual. The *Ka* is then 'wiped' and reformatted with the present ingrained core values of that individual, without past life memories, for subsequent integration with the next vessel chosen to house that entity.

Judgment

At death, when one's consciousness is released from the physical realm to the spiritual side (that continuum beyond physical time and space), that life is judged only by its own entity against the absolute universal values of Good and Evil, under Natural Law. Higher enlightened spirits or Masters assist each individual during this judgment process. One's consciousness is raised to its true enlightenment level, no longer limited in perception and understanding as in the tangible world. All elements of one's complete essence or soul, its combined *Ka* and *Ba*, are once again united. Earthly perspectives and false distortions are eliminated, allowing unbiased evaluations of one's actions undertaken during their most recent life, without being influenced by their physical senses. Self-assessment is then undertaken, with no other entity ever judging the thoughts, actions, or attitudes perpetrated by another individual during any mortal life.

Such self-judgment always results in absolute truth, without any prejudice or deceit. As individuals responsible for all our own deeds, we know the true intent of each and every one of our actions. Virtually, we can not lie to, or deceive ourselves. During this time of judgment, we utilize our fully expanded state of enlightenment, reflective of our cumulative and presently attained personal progress and achieved level of understanding. Our purpose is then to evaluate what has been learned; what faults and deficiencies yet remain (with recognition of any flaws that have been corrected); and determine the gain or loss in personal enlightenment achieved during the most recently completed physical existence.

It is illogical to believe that judgment for eternal salvation would ever be based upon only one lifetime of deeds, committed during merely a short span of time on Earth. Since the start of dynastic Egypt, it was believed that the gods or God would judge humans upon their death. This has persisted over the ages, and has been misinterpreted by most present religions of the world, and continues to be held as a misconception by many people. This misunderstanding involves the supposed final judgment by God of every

74

deceased entity's just expired life.

The earliest recorded form of this belief emerged from an ancient Egyptian notion wherein the god Osiris conducted a final judgment. But that actual Egyptian belief professed that all deceased humans reverted back to their original form, the 'spiritual form' of Osiris, the ethereal nature of the Godhead itself. Hence, the concept was actually 'Osiris judging Osiris' upon mortal death, or more correctly 'self-judging-self.' Such a process referred to each individual judging their own actions, since only that individual knew their true intent behind every past deed that they committed.

This correctly meant that each individual entity, when in spiritual form after the physical death of their most recent vessel, reviews or 'judges' their own just-expired life to determine the lessons that were learned and what remaining deficiencies still await correction. Such a process further exposes all the missed opportunities that went unused, which wasted at least some of that person's most recent life-path occasions to correct their remaining character deficiencies. This personal assessment of failed opportunities, along with specific gains and accomplishments made during that most recent life, further guides each entity on their continued path toward perfection, which ultimately leads to reunification with the Creator.

The one who actually committed those past deeds under review solely conducts this 'final' judgment. Truth would always result from such self-evaluation, since we can not deceive ourselves. Everyone would know the true motive and intent behind all their past actions. Such actions were either accidental ones, or deliberate acts; performed with the intent of being either hurtful or helpful.

Likewise, no one has the right to judge others. Another person may be achieving individual accomplishments at their best potential, at a rate of development unique to their specific ability. The scale used to measure such achievement is truly an individual one, since each entity is uniquely different. Since growth toward perfection and harmony is the ultimate desire, absolute truth will always prevail during this self-evaluation or judgment process of our present status. A realization or comprehension of one's still retained deficiencies and faults also comprises a part of this self-judgment process. During this evaluative procedure, we truly know ourselves. Comparisons are not made with others, since each entity is individually different, with their own unique and varying levels of achieved correction, growth, understanding, and enlightenment.

Ultimate Goal

By understanding that the intended purpose of physical existence is to learn, correct, contribute, and grow during repetitive cycles of experiencing life's lessons; our overriding goal should be to strive toward being the best person possible, always operating at our highest obtained level of achievement. Such an effort should be viewed as the seemingly proper way in which to live life, based solely on its own merit, rather than seeking some reward for its implementation. This goal must be undertaken without vanity or bitterness, which can emerge from comparison with others. There will always be greater and lesser levels of consciousness than ours, existing at any given time within the tangible realm. We create our own 'timetable' of achievement toward this ultimate goal of perfection, sometimes forcing actions and responses to life's events. Since every individual is different and hopefully advancing based upon their present capacity, progress appropriate for each entity will vary greatly, but in due time will ultimately occur.

While progress can be made toward one's goal while in the spiritual realm, it is within the physical world where we have the most opportunity for advancement, through our interactions with others. Simply stated, the material world offers more temptations and lessons from which we can learn.

Since it is impossible to accomplish all required correction of deficiencies and faults during a single lifetime in an attempt to perfect one's character, there exists a transcending and ultimate goal within the overall scope of both our physical and spiritual existence.

That ultimate goal is to obtain total acceptance of all living creatures, entities, and things. This is achieved by recognizing, correcting, and eliminating all negative traits, thereby gaining complete enlightenment and knowledge. Such an 'ultimate goal' toward complete perfection can only be achieved in individual steps or stages, through experiencing one's 'purpose lessons' or trials during mortal life. But one is expected to learn from those lessons, and correct the targeted character deficiencies in order to also progress spiritually. Such a step-by-step process continues in a cumulative manner from life to life, eventually replacing all negative behavioral traits with the desired 'Master' or perfected level. Such perfection is the ultimate goal of every entity, which results in complete and total peace, contentment, and harmony; the ultimate state of being.

Rewards

Within an individual's effort to achieve such goals, we should also allow time to experience and enjoy the rewards and pleasures offered by our material world, without abusing those gifts. There are countless rewards open to us on the earthly plane. Our physical senses allow each of us unique opportunities to experience these pleasures, which are not available within the spiritual realm. Too often, misguided and unimportant material distractions seem to consume our attention, prohibiting full appreciation of these ubiquitous gifts or rewards.

Perhaps love is the most important and rewarding gift available. Love is the innate adhesive force that binds relationships, on both the spiritual and physical planes. Love can only be given, never owned or possessed by another. Love must always be given freely, without expectations of anything in return, or with any conditions attached. Although love is perennial and transcends both the physical and spiritual planes, the tangible closeness associated with our physical senses is offered only within the mortal world. Love can provide certain unique elements and pleasures, along with an enhanced meaning to physical existence, within every corporeal life. Material goods are a further gift offered to us. Such tangible possessions, products, and devices provide comfort while extending human skills that aid physical life. But it is imperative to keep such rewards in proper perspective. *They are not the reason or purpose of life.* The real possessions of value are commodities we can take with us upon death, becoming a permanent part of each entity. Such qualities are then retained perpetually within both the spiritual and material realms. Those possessions include the intangible assets of love, tolerance, moral values, knowledge, and positive character traits. Basically, if one can not take a specific 'possession' with them into the spiritual realm for all of eternity, then it is likely of no true lasting value.

One's physical body is also a gift, although sometimes it can become a trial or a lesson. This gift expects certain 'compensation' in the form of productive contributions to the world, in return for its use. Minimal requirements necessitate keeping one's body healthy, presentable, clean, and protected from harm and injury. Expectations of what an individual may contribute to the world are based upon one's individually obtained potential, predicated on their currently achieved level of growth. More is always expected from those that have achieved higher abilities and enlightenment.

Such expectations continue to grow as one's physical capabilities also increase. Eternal rewards will surely result from productive use of our personal resources, through implementation of their positive impact on humanity, in both physical and emotional ways. We will ultimately judge ourselves on how well we used or abused our personal resources during mortal life.

Perhaps personal attitude is one of the most important ingredients necessary for a successful life. Focus on what each of us as unique individuals can control and accomplish, such as a personal objective to work hard, learn, be resilient, and remain optimistic. Never dwell on any perceived hardship or obstacle such as a difficult childhood, unfair treatment by authoritative figures, apparent 'bad luck,' or a seeming lack of opportunities. Life is unfolding as intended.

Focus on realistic goals that can be achieved through personal efforts, regardless of the environment or status in which we were born. Rise above such challenges, deriving strength from each step taken along that arduous climb from the depths of our earliest beginnings. As incremental goals are achieved, additional higher goals can then be sought. But never reach for unrealistic goals; all can not be rocket scientists, brain surgeons, or President of the United States.

Another of humanity's rewards is the beautiful planet we are allowed to inhabit, with all its natural bounty, scenery, resources, and animal and plant life. Again, such rewards come with a responsibility, as that of a caretaker. It is expected that humankind will care for and use Earth's resources and gifts in an intelligent manner. Things that are utilized must also be replenished, so that future generations, our reincarnated selves, will have the same opportunity for its enjoyment and future productive use. Since the world we inhabit is merely on temporary loan to all of us, any unwise utilization of this reward can have a potentially ironic twist. Those who now pollute, ravage, and exploit our planet, will also reincarnate here sometime in the future. They will return to a world of their own making to reap and suffer all the negative consequences of their prior misuse and abuse of these precious resources.

It is written that humankind is the master over the land,

seas, and 'lower' animals of Earth. Then as masters over Earth, we must be responsible for the use, care, and protection of all that is around us, not the exploitation of those resources with which we are entrusted. Rights possessed by humankind, which are also intertwined with the intelligent use of natural resources, end when they infringe upon the rights of those inherent 'gifts' to receive responsible treatment, protection, care, and utilization. Most specifically, any and all abuse or cruelty to animals must be recognized as a blatant offense to our world, as well as to our Creator.

The twentieth century personification of ethics, Dr. Albert Schweitzer (1875-1965), harbored a philosophy that espoused reverence for all life when he stated: "Ethics are complete, profound, and alive only when addressed to all living beings."[7] Ancient teachings by the Egyptian god, Thoth, further indicated that animals were on a separate evolutionary stream of enlightenment from that of humans; with certain branches of animals, such as dolphins and lions, thought to be on a higher evolutionary level than other animals. Humanity must respect all life as an integral part of this intended natural order.

Science indicates that the electroencephalograms (EEGs) of animals are analogous to those of humans, with the EEGs of primates such as gorillas being nearly indistinguishable from those of humans.[8] Animals, as sentient creatures similar to us, are just as likely to possess souls as are humans. They feel pain, communicate, and form communities within their social structures. They must also be allowed their right to a full and unencumbered existence. Humans, as the recognized superior intelligent beings of Earth, can not gain enlightenment without realizing that all life possesses real and specific value. Such respect and understanding must be reflected in our treatment of the lowest forms of life, and continue through all interactions with more complex creatures that share our planet; each having their distinct rights and intended purpose.

Assessment

The ability to recognize and understand the specific life-path lessons planned for our present physical existence may also be considered a unique gift. Such knowledge allows focus and effort to be concentrated on correction and subsequent change of our retained faults and deficiencies. This realization may become known to each individual through personal meditation, introspection, or self-realization of those shortcomings; as noted or observed from their personal responses toward events throughout life. Often times, comprehension of such deviant character or behavioral deficiencies can also be recognized during or shortly after a traumatic event or similar disruptive experience in life.

Recording a personal journal of actions and thoughts that transpired during disruptive or stressful times may be a helpful practice. From such a continuing critique of our responses and attitudes, a picture of our 'character composition' might start to emerge from those observations over a period of time. A periodic review of those records will often reveal a repetitive pattern of a specific negative behavioral trait. Such retained negative characteristics can then be recognized and corrected through one's conscious efforts. Too often we refuse to take responsibility for our actions and the resultant disorder they bring, by erroneously blaming others or even life itself. There is no better way to remain stagnant and depressed then to simply refuse to accept that we ultimately control our own life, all the while continuing to deny our own character deficiencies.

While self-assessment of our actions during our physical journey is a worthwhile endeavor, do not 'over-think' life. There is a difference between critiquing one's actions, and wallowing over perceived injustices in life. Never become bogged down by unfairness, it is an integral part of any existence. That is not to suggest that you should not defend your actions and positions when such inequities arise, but let them go after presenting your case concisely and clearly.

In such matters, it is of greatest importance to always be moving forward along your life-path...never permitting one's self to become trapped by life's unfairness. Do not dwell on such events, outcomes, or mistakes encountered during your 'formative years.' Once learning from those incidents, always move forward with your life. Never let temporary setbacks, individual defeats, unfair treatment, or inaccurate assertions derail your progress. There will be plenty of time after you have set forth your best effort, expended your 'youthful' energy, achieved your goals, concluded your career, achieved retirement, or otherwise completed your 'formative period' of development. At such time, it then becomes 'safe' to assess one's numerous failures and successes with more in-depth introspective analysis and assessment, without fear of adversely affecting one's intended life's mission. Any inappropriate dwelling over present or prior setbacks can often deter us from moving ahead with life as it was intended. Always grasp opportunities when presented; they emerge when we are ready to engage and confront them.

If one thinks they have been wrongly 'held-back' in their career, poorly treated or abused in a relationship, or perhaps fired unjustly or otherwise been unfairly manipulated; any continued dwelling over those events can often paralyze that person, consuming the energy necessary to move forward along their life path. Do not wallow in 'self-pity' over any unfair treatment you might encounter during your formative years. There will always be ample time later for such assessment when it will not act as a deterrent to your intended progress. Time always provides a clearer perspective, along with expanded objectivity, toward those more challenging lessons in life; ultimately allowing ensuing wisdom to be derived from those intended 'life-trials.'

Prices (Karma)

The freedom of choice granted by our inherent free will allows each of us to be in control of our own life, and hence our ultimate fate. Negative character behavior, such as intolerance toward others; judging others; or causing harm to others; all carry the price of negative karma. Karma is the universal law of cause-and-effect, the natural order of check-and-balance. Its universal implementation will eventually create harmony. As in nature, harmony always requires balance. As one builds negative karma from their retained character deficiencies, payment is eventually required through future good acts, to bring one's soul back into balance. We can not achieve our goal of perfection until individual deficiencies are corrected and replaced with positive attitudes and actions, with all past transgressions being 'repaid' and balanced through later 'good deeds.'

One of the greatest prices or penalties one can pay occurs as the result of wasting a lifetime in the physical world by refusing to learn life's planned lessons, thus negating any correction and subsequent growth in enlightenment. A closed mind, negative attitudes, and simple laziness are character traits that assure failure within this pursuit. Individuals perpetuating such irresponsible behavior can expect even more misery within successive lives, since drastic measures apparently are required to 'get their attention.' The prospect of future emptiness and unhappiness should serve as a catalyst to alter one's present perspective, thereby accepting responsibility to undertake the required character changes necessary to correct any retained faults, improving one's life.

Rejection or denial of love also carries a high price. Love seems to be one of the most difficult emotions for humanity to master. Communication is the key toward achieving this most precious resource. Misunderstandings, impatience, and imaginings are emotional deficiencies that isolate and prevent one from interacting and bonding with another. Pride, stubbornness, and ego, along with attempts to control another, often preclude love and happiness from our lives. The resulting loneliness and despair are high prices to pay for such negative behavior.

It is not by chance that couples meet. But love must be mutual to assure its success. Even if a complete and honest attempt for harmony is made within a relationship, negatives may still remain. That might result in one partner ending the relationship through exercise of their free will act of discernment, a right possessed by everyone. Then the other partner must accept that outcome as fate, as an exercise of choice by their companion, and ultimately end such a union.

Perhaps such a relationship was destined to fail, its purpose meant to serve only as a learning experience. Such a lesson might require reassessment of one's character, thereby discovering existing deficiencies that can then be addressed and corrected. Harboring resentment or bitterness toward the free will decision of another will always result in negative karma, and will create impediments towards personal growth. It should be realized that one-sided love is acceptable, since love transcends time, and a future encounter may yet await such 'soul mates' when improved conditions or enhanced enlightenment levels allow for better mutual compatibility.

The imbalance brought about by building negative karma separates us from harmony with the universe and creates a detour that keeps us from completing our purpose and goal in life. Prices must eventually be paid to bring us back in balance with the universe, back to the intended natural order. Not all prices are collected within the current lifetime. The price paid for past and present negative lifestyles may be many future existences spent in righting the wrongs done by those prior evil ways, along with wasting opportunities for any additional learning and growth.

As previously noted, mistakes will be repeated over and over until finally corrected. *There exists all the time in eternity to continually repeat unenlightened and unhappy lives until those retained deficiencies causing such misery are corrected, and our behavior is finally modified.* With true eternal contentment, happiness, and harmony waiting in our future, such stubborn resistance to positive change is a terribly high price to pay for delaying those rewards.

Taking of Life

Doing harm to others certainly results in negative karma, requiring future retribution before further enlightenment and growth may proceed. Of all humanity's indiscretions toward fellow man, murder appears to have the most severe consequence. Such an act not only ends the life of another prematurely, thereby denying their right to life, but also disrupts the natural order of the universe by negating intended fulfillment of that person's preset life-path events and potential accomplishments as planned. No one is allowed to interfere with developments in the ongoing cumulative learning efforts of another, which could potentially lead to their further growth and higher enlightenment. Such a disruption within this grand order is the most flagrant affront to the Creator. The most severe prices and retribution are demanded for this major transgression.

Harming one's self by ending our own life prematurely through suicide also carries grave implications. Since an individual's lessons are planned before birth, with no trial ever beyond our endurance or current capacity, such an act reflects weakness, surrender, and abandonment. It negates any correction and growth made during such a deliberately shortened life. The physical longevity of each life is established before birth, and must be fulfilled in its entirety; thereby allowing all planned lessons to occur. Typically, one argument attempting to 'defend' the act of suicide suggests that one should be judged for their entire life lived, not merely on the final few moments of that life. But that shows flawed reasoning, entirely dismissing the overall intent of

85

physical life, which is to learn, correct, contribute, and grow. Such an argument also ignores the remainder of life that was not allowed to be fulfilled, and those additional lessons that were planned to occur during that remaining time. Such 'lost' remaining life may have provided some of the best learning opportunities offered within that specific life-path existence.

A consciousness prematurely released to the spiritual side by suicide will always encounter confusion and fear, since the readiness of spiritual guides and the planning for such a return are in an unprepared state for such an unscheduled occurrence. The price for premature end is rebirth for whatever time remains unfulfilled from that previous life. That usually results in a 'young' physical death in one's subsequent life. Such an early departure may end a richly rewarding 'future life,' while causing grief in other lives affected by that shortened existence. Such a diminished subsequent life also allows little or no opportunity for happiness, learning, growth through correction, or gain in enlightenment. Moreover, the previous life's lessons must be relearned in their entirety; plus the addition of 'new' lessons to correct the deficiencies of weakness, surrender, and defeat, which were underlying influences that precipitated the suicide action.

The price of suicide is not merely 'starting over,' but also involves a 'setback' or reduction in enlightenment from one's previous level. That reduction becomes an additional delay towards one's ultimate goal. Much time is wasted, other lives are affected, and further suffering is always required, since one must still confront and master the learning event or lesson that originally prompted the suicide. One's physical and mental state are taken into account during self-judgment of such action, but certain prices must still be paid to eventually balance karma.

Chapter Five

Theology

With a basic comprehension of fundamental concepts and terms from the preceding chapter, various tenets can be formulated into a number of cohesive beliefs. The term 'theology' refers to those collections of coherent and rational philosophies that pertain to the supreme Godhead. It encompasses the general study of the divine, and attributes of God, along with the relationship between the divine and our physical universe. According to most religious beliefs, there is only one universal and supreme Godhead, the Creator.

Yet this Supreme Source is known by many different names within the diversity of our various religious beliefs. Thus, all religions are apparently diverse expressions referring to the same Creator, although defined through different perceptions held by the followers of each faith. Yet the majority of differences separating many organized religions exist only within the individual ceremonies and rituals that are followed by each religious belief. Doctrine pertaining to the Creator, along with the notion that one should live an ethical and virtuous life, are integral parts of most religions, with many differences often found merely within more insignificant areas of each diverse faith.

Perhaps the greatest theological difficulty emerges from the use of the term 'God.' Any reference to God seems to invoke a specific but often different Supreme Being within each separate religious belief, conjuring up multiple concepts of numerous dissimilar deities. But when the term 'Creator' is substitute for 'God,' nearly everyone is left with the same impression or concept. The very act of humans assigning a name to the Creator seems to denote a possible tangible distinction between the variously named deities of each specific religious faith. But such differentiation seems to disappear when the word 'Creator' is used. The Creator is universally thought to be the supreme and unseen force responsible for the creation of our physical universe. No further designation or description seems to be necessary in order to identify that Supreme Entity.

Ancient manuscripts seem to indicate that 'God' may actually be a lesser deity than the Creator. The original Hebrew belief worshipped only one God, Yahweh, but recognized other gods worshipped by surrounding 'neighboring' nations. The Christian faith acknowledges two personifications: God the Father (often associated with the Hebrew God Yahweh) and God the Son, Jesus. Additionally, Christianity combines those two Gods with a nebulous, non-corporeal third entity, the Holy Ghost or Spirit; thereby forming a Holy Trinity comprised of three separate entities combined within a single Supreme Godhead.

Believing in something so strongly that one is willing to forfeit their physical life does not alter the factual reality of what actually exists. The death of martyrs within a specific faith does not prove the factual reality of their individual belief. That concept can best be demonstrated by prevailing convictions seen during the Dark Ages, when most of the greatest scientific minds, along with the Church Fathers and leaders, virtually 'knew' that our flat Earth was at the center of a universe of very limited size. However, such a strong belief did not change the factual reality of a spherical Earth that, along with other neighboring planets, circled a central star; all comprising a small portion within an average galaxy, which is located within an unremarkable part of a vastly larger universe.

In his *Lectures on the Science of Religion*, F. Max Müller expressed that: "Men fight about religion on Earth; in heaven they shall find out that there is only one true religion...the worship of God's Spirit."[1]   Apparently oral traditions pertaining to Earth's earliest spiritual veneration were repeatedly interpreted incorrectly throughout history. Those numerous distortions have helped to suppress the body of knowledge known as the *Ancient Wisdom* that once prevailed on Earth, which is thought to have been imparted to humanity by emissaries of the Creator. Evidence further indicates that certain groups continued to suppress those ancient truths throughout later centuries, thereby promoting their own political agenda.

Humans have acknowledged some form of Higher Power since primordial times. Such an ultimate entity, an all-powerful source from which everything emerged, was recognized as the Creator, an unseen entity that remained incomprehensible and formless. That Entity has been called many names, such as All-Maker, The Supreme, The One, and The Source. Colonel James Churchward revealed that an ancient *Naga* copy of the *Sacred Naacal Writings* that was found in India claimed that the Creator was 'incomprehensible,' and as such could not be named or described. Hence, the Creator was known as the Nameless in that writing.[2]   The use of the human term *God* was a relatively later occurrence, and may have started as a description for other superior physical beings that were considered to be above humans, but below the Creator.

Still later, the meaning of the word 'God' came to represent Earth's unseen highest deity, and even later still, the term 'God' came to denote the Creator. Such nomenclature invokes an image of a physical being, which may be erroneous. Pure energy would need neither shape nor a vessel in which to exist, and would be more restrained in any physical form than in a pure energy state.

The oldest human references to a Supreme Being were those clearly describing the Creator. A personification of the 'ancient gods' did not emerge until after *c.*3350 BC, perhaps due to a lack of differentiation between the Creator and

89

certain later physical beings who displayed superhuman abilities. That marked the transference of divinity from the ethereal to the physical realm, although the One and Only Creator would have no reason to confine Its (gender being unnecessary for 'spiritual' entities) essence within a physical vessel. Most extant original texts, which were not subjected to later revisionist alterations, clearly concede that none of those ancient gods could have been the Creator, the ultimate Supreme Entity. References contained in Christian Gnostic texts are perhaps the most specific statements reflecting that assertion.

Mention of a Supreme Deity in Earth's most archaic records only referred to that Force as the 'Creator,' an entity that ancient people did not call 'God,' but merely 'The Creator.' The term *God* simply appears to be a much later classification devised by humanity, with its meaning being altered or augmented numerous times over the ages. The Greek term *dios*, meaning 'god,' was derived from the Sanskrit word *div*, meaning 'bright or shining.' Perhaps the later evolution of divinity emerged from humankind's attempt to explain and elevate certain other physical beings to a higher level of adoration, influence, or power.

The concept of a universal Godhead was first recorded in the *Pyramid Texts* of Egypt, with its oldest extant reference dated to *c.*2500 BC, one believed to be a reaffirmation of an even earlier record from *c.*3100 BC, although its origins definitely date to predynastic times before written records. That hierarchical concept is known as *The Lineage of Horus*, which reveals a group of nine gods called the Ennead, which included: Shu, Tefnut, Geb, Nut, Osiris, Isis, Seth, Nephthys, and Horus.[3] But that lineage also revealed a tenth god, Atum. According to the *Pyramid Texts*, Atum is the Very Old One, the One, the Oldest One, the Lord of All, the Great One, and the Primeval One, with Atum meaning: "...the one who has been completed by absorbing others."[4]

Atum was born before heaven, Earth, the gods, humans,

and before anything else came into existence. Atum was also the concept of the first living beings, the *Divine Ones*, from which the genealogy of the gods emerged. Such a definition implies that those divine ancestors were not gods themselves, but their later lineage or descendants evidently became 'gods.' Other specific references to the Creator appeared throughout the *Pyramid Texts*, claiming the Creator was "He whose name is not known,"[5] the Highest Entity within our universe.

God eventually became the term used by later humans when referring to the Creator. After an initially long duration during which the Supreme Entity was known only as the Creator, the terms 'God' and 'Creator' apparently became interchangeable, referring to the same Divine Entity. Sometime between those two distinct periods, a physical God or group of gods reigned over Earth. Apparently such ancient divine beings became the supreme Gods described by the various beliefs comprising each of our different major religions, as well as certain gods of mythological accounts.

Many ancient accounts record periodic changes in either a sole God, or in leadership over a collective group of gods. Yet those records seemingly suggest a distinct difference between God and the Creator. The personification of those ancient divine beings was in the image and likeness of humans, or *vice versa*, depending on one's perspective. Certain humans were even thought to be descendants of those divine beings, producing myths stating that humankind had been created by various acts performed by those gods or God. Numerous other myths proposed that man had been formed from the dust or clay of Earth. The idea that humans were brought into existence from 'clay' first appeared in Egypt around 2000 BC, as an act performed by their 'creator god,' Khnum. Still later, that concept again emerged within the Old Testament of the Hebrew Bible.

However, any anthropomorphic personification of the Creator is simply illogical, since the Creator must be above all human frailties and faults. The linking of the human

91

image with the Supreme Entity was more likely humanity's own elevation of their ancient ancestors, which were often raised to the level of deities upon their death, perhaps as a sign of reverence for their part as role models. The Greek philosopher, Xenophanes (*c*.540 BC) emphatically stated that the "greatest God..." resembled mankind "...neither in form nor in mind."[6]

A sole Universal Deity, the Godhead, is a principle, an abstract idea or belief not of concrete finite form. Even with the unknowable aspect of the Creator, most philosophers and many theologians believe that only a limited knowledge of the Creator is even possible, due to the very nature of such a nebulous concept and lack of basis for Its comprehension. Any rationale for such a speculative assumption might emerge from mystical experiences, visions, revelations, or even from a sense of nearby 'presence.' Perhaps renowned mythologist Joseph Campbell best defined humanity's concept of God, describing God as a metaphor for a mystery that absolutely transcends all human categories of comprehension or thought.[7] Thus, God becomes a creation of man, shaping God into humanity's notion of what a Supreme Entity or Higher Power should be.

But the Creator was never a male or female of any one race or ethnicity, nor a physical form of any particular species. Thus, a specific gender reference or physical description of any Supreme Being undoubtedly refers to some lesser divinity or god. By any name, there is only one Creator. However, the human term 'god' could be personalized, becoming any gender, assuming any form, and could be known by any number of various names. Such a reference could even refer to a being of a different physical species.

God is an individual concept of personal belief, but the concept of the Creator is universal. Any religious debate as to the true and factual nature of the Creator would not directly alter the true essence of the Creator. Such debate would merely affect certain religious followers and participants, perhaps modifying their individual belief or concept of such a Supreme Entity. The consequence from other similar misconceptions would also have no direct affect on factual reality, regardless of the eloquence of its debate. Such arguments often merely create a 'God' for each participant, merely assigning one's personal image to their reality of such a Supreme Entity. Regardless, the intent of any spiritual belief should be to instill purpose and direction throughout life. Such belief should provide the strength, inspiration, and desire to cope with physical existence, while providing reassurance and comfort that mortal life is unfolding and developing as it should.

The Creator is the power from which all lifeforce energy emanates. Additionally, such a central dynamic force may also be the source of collective consciousness throughout the entire universe. In macro-combination, all things within the universe may be 'components' of the Creator, with the limitless boundaries of the universe forming the Creator's containment vessel. Such a concept may encompass the belief that the universe is a single organism, comprised of many 'life-cells,' with each life-cell being the individual entity known as one's soul. The sum of all the souls would then constitute the 'component parts' of the whole, thereby forming that central lifeforce energy known as the Creator.

If correct, we are all a distinct and individual part of the Creator, with no beginning or end. We are all 'one' with the universe. We could think of our essence as a single cosmic molecule collectively comprising the framework of the Creator, just as each cell or molecule within every corporeal body comprises one's own mortal being. Similar to a single cell within the physical body becoming cancerous, each individual 'cosmic cell' or soul would also affect the rest of its cosmic framework comprising the totality of the Creator. One's individual actions similarly affect everything else within the physical universe, either glorifying the whole or degrading it.

The universe itself may be a manifestation of the primordial energy force that created the existence of matter and space-time. Both matter and space-time are components of the physical universe, while the spiritual component, our eternal souls, might provide the lifeforce energy to animate each corporeal vessel. Hence, we are each a finite and integral part of the universal consciousness that pervades both realms, utilizing mortal lives to initiate correction and gain knowledge through learning from our 'life-experiences,' while increasing individual enlightenment. There exists a finite underlying and silent connection with every thought and action that occurs throughout the entire physical universe. Our deeds intertwine and affect all other events within the cosmos, with all events and souls apparently somehow instantaneously connected.

Eternal energy comprises each consciousness, which can also be described as our spirit or soul. Such energy can not be destroyed, only reshaped or changed. The physical realm supplies an unlimited number of bodies to house this nebulous essence life-after-life, for continued enlightenment and contribution to the universe. Physical life is a continuous first-run film, with an abundance of future sequels. As one experiences physical life and achieves ever-greater awareness through higher enlightenment, their energy level increases, resulting in an enhanced state of being. One's capabilities and potential are then amplified through such energy increases.

The Creator, as well as the entire universe, requires contributions from all individual parts working in harmony within the physical realm in order to create its necessary balance. The universe is too orderly, symmetrical, and interwoven to have been random in origin. One's individual growth, acquired through learning and correction, along with one's accomplishments, then represent individual contributions to the whole, in either a positive or negative way. Such contributions help maintain order and balance within our universe, or undermine it with chaos.

Since we are all an independent but integral part of the universe, whatever we do glorifies or degrades the whole, as well as ourselves individually. As we ultimately grow, our consciousness expands towards its highest state of enlightenment. Through humanity's individual as well as our cumulative achieved progress, every one of us can eventually obtain the ultimate highest level, the Master Level of perfection, thereby acquiring complete acceptance, knowledge, and peace.

Perfection

Perfection is the evolution toward a central point, a return back to its original source. If all physical objects were fragments of the Creator, with each element representing an individual portion, such return must first be 'perfected' prior to reunification. Such fragmentation of the Creator is thought to have occurred during the initial energy release of the Big Bang event.

Some believe that the Creator spent an eternity as only a single point source; or perhaps numerous eternities, if such spans of time are possible. Such a concept further proposes that the initiation of the Big Bang event was an evolution away from that singular point of existence, an event that occurred from the Creator's isolation and loneliness. The Creator thus 'recreated' Itself through the energy release of the Big Bang event.

Physical evolution and eventual emanation of intelligence apparently emerges in measured and incremental stages. Individual enlightenment seems to emerge in a similar fashion, from bits and pieces exposed throughout mortal life. That permits each of us to obtain a certain level of self-awareness toward our duty of perfection, allowing eventual reunification with our Source. An awareness of such a relationship between self and our unseen Creator is necessary for such an evolution, one that recognizes our origin from that same fundamental authority or power. Perhaps the Creator experiences physical existence through the vicarious events of Its later creations, with an all-encompassing acceptance and knowledge as an underlying theme. Since all things in the physical world are apparently parts or portions of the Creator, such an Omniscient Source is thus able to actually experience life through the many diverse objects It has created.

Any reunification with the Creator would require each individual essence to acquire an infinite expansion of perception, an ability to perceive the 'whole' of existence. Such a fusion or joining with the Creator would therefore also require the correction or elimination of any acquired or retained faults. Such deficiencies would have been characteristics acquired over lengthy periods of time, from experiences involving numerous lifetimes of existence. Such acquired character flaws would therefore also require certain learning and correction in order to reach that desired ultimate level of perfection. Such continuing development and evolution of character would eventually allow each individual to correctly perceive the true reality of the physical world, while also achieving a level of acceptance and love beyond the self-interests of any single entity.

From such a Master Level of perfection, one's remaining purpose and obligation would be to guide and assist in the enlightenment and self-assessment process of other souls, those at a level lower than such Masters. There would be no need for Masters to experience further physical lives, since all would had been experienced, learned, and mastered. The sole purpose of any corporeal reincarnation from the Master Level would then be as an 'object lesson' or 'teacher' from which others might learn. Such a Master might choose to return for incarnation as a handicapped or deformed child, or an instructor, or perhaps a prophet. The reincarnation of a Master entity would truly be an act of pure love and acceptance of others, never a sacrifice.

As we continue through multiple lives, our transcendent goal is to strive for obtainment of that Master Level of perfection, through continued learning, understanding, and achieving three prime objectives, which are known as Universal Constants:

1. To tolerate, leading to full acceptance of all other things and beings within the universe. To avoid being judgmental, since one may only judge their own life within their achieved level of understanding, enlightenment, and frame of reference.
2. To expand one's consciousness, thereby raising their spiritual level of enlightenment through attainment of total knowledge and understanding of all that exists.
3. To recognize that all things and beings are developing as intended, while also appreciating their individual contributions and worth regardless of their 'level' of obtainment in either the physical or spiritual realm, thus promoting universal harmony and order.

When conscious omniscience is collectively achieved over untold many lifetimes of learning, correction, and growth, the Master Level is then obtained as one's individual reward of mastering total acceptance and full enlightenment. That achievable and desirable condition represents complete perfection, the ultimate goal towards which we all strive. Eternal contentment, happiness, and harmony can then become a perpetual reality.

Negative Forces

A belief in 'Good' requires an equal belief in 'Evil,' nature's balance and ironic dualism paradox. Evil is real, it does exist, as evidenced by the atrocities documented throughout Earth's historic record. Some believe that evil might start with jealousy, perhaps emerging from simple feelings of inferiority. If allowed to grow, jealousy can then manifest into hatred. When permitted to become an obsession, such hatred becomes violent, allowing one to derive pleasure from such vicious acts, thus creating true evil.

Yet evil is not from where any individual first started. At the original start of each personal reincarnation process, with one's initial birth, everyone emerged from a 'neutral point,' equal distance from both Good and Evil. Through exercise of free will choice, we either move toward the 'negative' or the 'positive' aspects of life. Evil is the commodity from which we must move, distancing us from its influence. It is the single greatest impediment that is encountered during each life-path, and is always counter-productive to all our needs, desires, and purpose.

Evil can manifest itself in many forms. Although always dark, foul, and hideous in its true state, it may deceive us cloaked in appeal, hiding its real appearance and purpose. Evil is an affront to all our sensibilities. Yet it draws us to it by promising rewards, short cuts, and an easy path in life. It is sometimes defined as the Seven Deadly Sins, which include Pride, Lust, Covetousness, Anger, Gluttony, Envy, and Sloth. However, it certainly also includes other negative traits such as vanity, arrogance, irresponsibility, impatience, dominance, selfishness, vindictiveness, ignorance, and cruelty, as well as assorted criminal activities and intentions.

Constant vigilance is required to recognize Evil for its true purpose, which is to decay, use, corrupt, control, destroy, and avert us from our purpose and goal in life. Caution must always be exercised during daily life to recognize Evil in its many forms and avoid its negative influence.

If, indeed, the universe is the creation of a single primordial lifeforce energy in the form of a Supreme Entity, the reality of Good and Evil seems to reflect the ultimate paradox. Such a contradiction focuses on the enigmatic reason why that Supreme Entity would intend for Good to come forth, yet also allow Evil to exist (or for that matter, why create the annoying mosquito?). But the Creator did not create Good or Evil. Just as Good is a product of the physical realm, Evil manifests from negative acts committed while in the material world. Both commodities are products associated with physical life, with every individual allowed choices in either direction, along their own path toward ultimate perfection. The Creator never imposes Its will on any mortal life, since free will choice was granted to everyone. Rather, the physical realm is the stage on which all conceivable actions, either righteous or debased, have been, are, or will eventually be transacted; thereby ultimately supplying the Creator with all knowledge, both good and bad, during the process. The devil does not tempt us. Rather, our own human weakness provides opportunities for temptations, allowing each individual to either reject or act upon those enticements. But any life-path can be altered, allowing change in direction with each future free will choice.

It would appear that the universe simply permits both Good and Evil to coexist, allowing for free will choice. Such a commingling of opposing elements appears to be as natural as predator and prey, or progress and decay; nature's ever present balance. The Supreme Entity that created all things simply does not interfere with any individual soul's development, or its specific direction toward either Good or Evil. Perhaps Evil simply emerged by its own design and intent, or it may be an elemental part of the underlying universe itself.

The originally neutral entity we acknowledge as our consciousness, soul, or spirit is simply allowed to evolve toward either Good or Evil, depending on our individual choice. Free will choice always exists, without any influence from a Higher Power ever exerting control or influence over such an individual developmental process. The evolution toward either of two diverging paths appears to produce the balance necessary within the universe. Similarly, while two opposing poles of magnets attract each other, perhaps Good and Evil draw together the cohesive fabric of our universe, while also separating those two commodities, in a manner similar to the repulsion of magnetic 'like-poles.' Hence, Good and Evil might be an integrated set of natural forces, both providing cohesion and balance within our physical universe.

When a consciousness obtains its perfected energy state at the Master Level, that soul then stops its continuing cycle of incarnation. It then merges with other perfected energy of its own kind, either Good or Evil, dependent upon its chosen path as a collective part of such auspicious power. Perfected or Pure Evil is very different from the perfected Good of the Master Level; since no temptation or false promise could ever exist that would entice, influence, or corrupt Pure Good. Pure Evil utilizes only temptation and fear, although it always delights in the spread of suffering and brutality throughout our physical realm.

Throughout life, occurrences can arise that produce foreboding consequences. One's mental state and degree of metaphysical awareness, as well as exposure to hypnotic sessions, occult practices, or other psychic phenomena have reportedly resulted in contact with forces beyond our normal comprehension, seemingly defying physical explanations. Caution should be exercised when dealing with such connections or channels that might create a link between the earthly plane and the spiritual realm. Like any door or corridor when opened, it may allow both welcomed contact and communication, or conversely permit unwanted energy to gain access through that same opening.

Negative forces associated with elements of Evil apparently exist; emanating from perfected evil within the spiritual realm, or from acts committed within the mortal world. They seemingly await any opportunity to contact us, thus gaining control and influence over our actions. Pure Evil goes beyond an absence of empathy for others, deriving enjoyment from inflicting pain and suffering at every opportunity. Pure Evil lacks both conscience and compassion, and is gratified by the suffering of others. Affirmation of positive thoughts may provide some protection during negative encounters, but it is best to simply avoid any situation harboring such evil influences.

Religion

Humanity's organized religions of today are just that: religions organized by humans. The early forms of religious belief, along with their corresponding deities, appear to have been created by our ancient ancestors to provide simple explanations for inexplicable physical occurrences. As more traditional religious beliefs emerged, humanity's emphasis shifted from the physical aspect of existence, to genuine concern with the well being or salvation of our spiritual component. A fundamental belief in a single universal Higher Power then emerged. Such a metaphysical concept was apparently imparted to early cultures by higher divine beings, since such abstract concepts are not something that would be self-evident to an evolving culture of primitive people.

Over the millennia, religious translations of earlier testaments, prophetic pronouncements, and associated underlying doctrines have been modified, making those original beliefs agree with a certain few who benefited from those changes. Many contemporary religious institutions seem to have lost their altruistic intent and purpose. In some instances, church hierarchy has replaced earlier doctrine with a specific political agenda, in order to manipulate and coerce the gullible in a deliberate effort to redistribute the wealth of its followers.

Such altered beliefs apparently first started during ancient times, when an anthropomorphic deity was concerned both with the type of an 'acceptable' sacrifice, as well as how it was killed.[8] Such pettiness and lack of empathy seems to

101

indicate that such a deity, one designated by its religious leaders, was more interested in dictating every action its followers made. Such control was administered directly by the leaders of those religions, superimposing their own agenda upon their followers in order to manipulate and control the unenlightened. Religious reverence and belief in the Creator must involve more than that. Even a few Christian denominations have replaced some of Jesus' original teachings with their own radical political agendas.

Some organized religions now predominantly preach a 'fear of God,' demanding money and control over its followers. Such modern religions have simply evolved into big businesses. In the United States alone, religious organizations receive tax-free donations exceeding fifty billion dollars annually, accounting for approximately one-half of all charitable contributions made. That money was collected by more than three thousand different and separate religious belief systems. Still, traditional organized religions appear to be necessary institutions. They serve a finite purpose, providing a basis or framework for proper thoughtfulness and righteous behavior.

Organized religion provides an essential starting point, the teaching of basic values of Good over Evil, with knowledge replacing ignorance. Wisdom might also result, or perhaps emerge as a by-product from one's normal search for deeper spiritual meaning and guidance within ordinary life. While organized religions may be a faster way to secure such wisdom, they often falter in supplying tangible answers and direction to life's more complex dilemmas and needs.

Religion may even act somewhat as a detriment, at least with certain individuals, by actually diminishing the notion that one is complete responsibility for all their own actions, as well as their individual salvation. As we gain knowledge and enlightenment while seeking further and deeper direction and meaning, perhaps we tend to outgrow these 'organized' religions.

As with funerals, modern religions are commodities for the living. They primarily serve the physical elements of life, not its spiritual component. Certain doubt might exist with the ability of organized religions to ultimately transcend from the material plane to the ethereal realm. Religion would seem to have limited importance within the spiritual world, due to its lack of emphasis on individual responsibility. Perhaps such disparity or disengagement exists as a result of one's perspective becoming altered by their physical senses while within the material world. Religion is never a passport or ticket to salvation. Rather, it is merely a compass, setting an intended course and direction. The actual effort is still left to each individual, requiring each of us to follow the correct path through all of life's intended lessons.

If a specific religious belief provides comfort and incentive for development of positive character traits, steering one towards Good rather than Evil, then it has accomplished its purpose. Within any religion, as in school or any other educational setting, one eventually learns what is being taught and graduates. Individuals reach a point where right and wrong, good and evil are understood concepts. Continued lectures simply become redundant, reinforcing what has already been exposed and taught. One must then proceed with the task of living, overcoming additional trials by learning life's latest lessons, while progressing toward further correction and growth.

A fallacy held by followers of certain organized religions is their myopic conviction that only their way of thought, action, and worship will result in salvation. They contend that only their beliefs and manner of worship are proper ways in which to live. One must question the value of any religious belief espousing such a closed-minded perspective of intolerance, rigid judgmental thought, and persecution of others. Regardless of one's religious beliefs, coping with daily life and interacting with others is a universal constant. Any belief should impart within its follower the desire to

103

strive to be the best one can be within their attained ability, contributing to the betterment of the world, while understanding and accepting everything around them. It would appear that a totally secular culture or nation could not survive the test of time. But that does not necessarily imply that a specific religion or religious belief is necessary for the longevity of those civilizations. In fact, organized religions formed by mortal beings have been consistently found to be insufficient over time, as they fail in their attempt to describe the indescribable: the Creator. Too often, religions formed by one group are at odds with competing beliefs, focusing attention on promoting their specific religion rather than on the importance of building a spiritual connection with the Creator. Too often such competition has an opposite effect, resulting in warfare between different religious factions. One should not solely consider the 'correctness' of any religious belief, but also the intent of its teachings. Competing beliefs need not be adversarial. Harm or condemnation should never result from teaching ethical values.

The purpose of any belief should be to establish personal responsibility for correction and growth, leading to the perfection of each entity. However, one can be spiritual without being religious. In fact, negatives can exist within certain religious beliefs that become addictive. That can impart great stress upon an individual, resulting in guilt and confusion over such rigid views and perceived human failures. Further, blind acceptance of any religious belief can eliminate our own responsibility for personal salvation. Individual perfection or ultimate salvation should not be things we relinquish to others. Rather, they must be achieved through one's individual efforts and actions of learning and correction. No one is going to save us from ourselves.

The concept of reincarnation provides an alternate creed and way-of-life philosophy, one different from more conventional beliefs. It answers certain questions, while supplying true purpose and goals in life. Reincarnation does not preach fear, nor does it promise short cuts or fads in coping with life. It does offer understanding; espousing tolerance, learning, correction, and ultimately growth, while also urging individual productivity at one's presently achieved capacity. It forces no penalty for mistakes, only the price of repeating lessons until each assignment is eventually learned through tests we are allowed to take over and over until passing; without ever failing or burning in hell. It promises no utopian lounging in heaven without purpose or duties, but rather continued contributions through assisting others from the Master Level, while also enjoying eternal peace and harmony achieved through one's own effort.

Reincarnation threatens no punishment, only assessment and evaluation by one's self. A process that instills both an intimate understanding and a desire for further improvement. It offers real purpose in physical life, as well as a tangible eternal goal; not abstract thoughts or ambiguous rewards. The uniqueness of each individual being, the result of humankind's varying enlightenment levels, requires different plateaus of guidance, knowledge and direction; not 'blind faith,' or a one-answer-fits-all approach. Reincarnation simply fulfills our spiritual needs, while supplying justification and fairness within every aspect of physical life.

Many fundamental teachings of organized religions are also similar beliefs within the concept of reincarnation. One learns to live by a universal code of conduct, the *Golden Rule*, which can influence and govern every behavior. It is a basic desire to do only good, thus defeating evil, while accomplishing positive deeds throughout earthly life that can result in future benefits. It is also the belief in a spiritual realm, one separate and beyond our known physical world, where an eternal ethereal life exists after corporeal death. Such an existence results in perpetual contentment and harmony within that realm of the Creator, regardless of how one might conceive such a domain or that Supreme Entity.

Reincarnation also professes a finite purpose in life, and the fairness of dispensed justice within the spiritual realm. It is the contentment and knowledge that the universal law of karma is always ultimately equitable, whether now or in the future. Although ensuing actions made as a result of our free will choice might result in certain mistakes, those same misdeeds can also be rectified or balanced through our own efforts of subsequent retribution, permanently offsetting and correcting those deficiencies and transgressions. The belief in reincarnation provides motivation, understanding, and direction throughout mortal life.

Each of us sets our individual timetable for correction and growth, which eventually leads to self-perfection and perpetual harmony. Reincarnation supplies a discipline and incentive not unlike certain aspects of conventional religions, but with an alternate concept and process toward ultimate salvation and unity with the Creator. It stresses personal responsibility while perhaps exposing true understanding of some of life's many mysteries.

Summary

Our purpose in a seemingly chaotic world is to learn life's lessons, thereby identifying and correcting negative behavioral traits. Success from that endeavor also promotes growth in spiritual enlightenment through the cumulative acquisition of knowledge and wisdom. When encountering life's destined events, a positive and honest interaction with all living things will offer abundant opportunities for individual learning and growth. Through such interaction, in conjunction with free will choice, mutual benefits may emerge for all involved, potentially supplying opportunities for personal perfection. Others can benefit from those same encounters and interactions, either directly as beneficiaries of such deeds, or from the example set by their positive consequences.

Cautious use of discernment allows avoidance of others who are negative influences, which could divert us from our mission in life. Recognize and accept that every person is individually different, each operating at their own greater or lesser level of developed growth and subsequent enlightenment. Awareness of that reality precludes comparison with others, or the temptation to judge others.

Positive interactions with others, along with all accomplishments made during ordinary life, however small or humble those contributions might be, improve and enhance the harmony within our universe. Discretion and caution should be exercised in identifying and dealing with all forms of evil and its trickery. But do not become cynical, since goodness can always be found. Negative attitudes will always hinder us from accomplishing our purpose in life. Each of us should strive to always be the best we can presently be, based on our current level of attainment derived from prior correction of deficiencies. But also be mindful of any remaining character flaws that still require transformation. Acknowledgment of those retained faults allows each of us to know our true self. Such humble recognition and personal evaluation also grounds us in reality, while helping to keep us accessible and receptive to others.

Rewards are abundant in life, with love the most precious gift. Know yourself and learn to accept and give love, without any false motives or intentions. Although love is perennial and an ever-attainable reward; personal perspective, ego, and imaginings can often deter its obtainment. As we mature and gain wisdom from life's lessons, we must endeavor to abandon our prior immature and frivolous ways. That transition can instill new meaning to life and provide understanding of our true mortal purpose. Such personal growth helps develop our core character, while also imparting wisdom. That enlightenment can then nurture the inner-strength necessary to shelter and comfort our spirit during times of disruption and unexpected misfortune.

We must prevent fear and distress from overcoming and controlling our life, either through imaginings or distorted perceptions. By assessing our present abilities and potential in a realistic manner, we can set practical goals and aspirations. Recognize that perseverance and patience will eventually produce the character traits, abilities, and goals desired. Each new improvement then builds upon all incremental steps previously made, moving ever closer toward eventual perfection. Such character changes, along with its ensuing growth, can then be utilized to confront and overcome future obstacles encountered along our intended life-path.

We are all individually part of the Creator and hence the universe; undoubtedly growing and developing as destined. Universal harmony emerges from the cumulative enlightenment produced from all individual learning and correction, resulting in serenity and balance that better equips all of us to cope with life's trials and lessons. Maintaining balance throughout life eliminates internal turmoil, thereby allowing an open mind and positive awareness of all that surrounds us.

Dedicated pursuit of our ultimate goal of perfection will eventually result in eternal harmony and contentment. Until then, exercise caution in life. Rely on your presently obtained level of development and wisdom, while faithfully listening to your 'inner-voice,' always performing at your highest level of presently attained capability. With careful purpose and deliberation, always strive to embrace happiness whenever it appears.

The essence of the preceding summary is most eloquently expressed in the following poem, *DESIDERATA*, penned by an unknown author in 1692, when it was originally found in Old Saint Paul's Church in Baltimore, Maryland. Similarities between the preceding summary and the following poem were indeed intentional.

DESIDERATA

Go placidly amid the noise & haste & remember what peace there may be in silence. As far as possible without surrender be on good terms with all persons. Speak your truth quietly & clearly; and listen to others, even the dull & ignorant; they too have their story. Avoid loud & aggressive persons, they are vexations to the spirit. If you compare yourself with others, you may become vain & bitter; for always there will be greater & lesser persons than yourself. Enjoy your achievements as well as your plans. Keep interested in your own career, however humble; it is a real possession in the changing fortunes of time. Exercise caution in your business affairs; for the world is full of trickery. But let this not blind you to what virtue there is; many persons strive for high ideals; and everywhere life is full of heroism. Be yourself. Especially, do not feign affection. Neither be cynical about love; for in the face of all aridity & disenchantment it is perennial as the grass. Take kindly the counsel of the years, gracefully surrendering the things of youth. Nurture strength of spirit to shield you in sudden misfortune. But do not distress yourself with imaginings. Many fears are born of fatigue & loneliness. Beyond a wholesome discipline, be gentle with yourself.

You are a child of the universe, no less than the trees & the stars; you have a right to be here. And whether or not it is clear to you, no doubt the universe is unfolding as it should. Therefore be at peace with God, whatever you conceive Him to be, and whatever your labors & aspirations, in the noisy confusion of life keep peace with your soul. With all its sham, drudgery & broken dreams, it is still a beautiful world. Be careful. Strive to be happy.

---Author Unknown

PART TWO

REINCARNATION

AS A WAY OF LIFE

Chapter Six

Perspective

The first part of this book attempted to define terms, correct misconceptions, and reveal fundamentals of the reincarnation process. But knowledge without a practical application is of little use. Hence, this book's second part will reveal how an understanding of reincarnation can be utilized to deal with life's difficulties; stressing the importance of proper perspective, choice, individual change, balance, and personal responsibility as key factors. This section is not presented as a guide to proper behavior, nor intended to gauge what may be right or wrong, passing judgment on any specific action. Rather, its intent is to expose the positive effects that an understanding of the reincarnation process can impart to each of us, revealing useful information for coping with daily life. The objective is to open our perception, allowing each of us to view the world within the full scope of eternity's 'larger picture,' thereby allowing better decisions and interactions to be made throughout mortal life.

Such a philosophy also relates to the ancient cosmological conviction of a divine Cosmic Order that was introduced in Chapter Three, which served as the ancient model for day-to-day living.[1] That prehistoric pattern or way-of-life provided direction and purpose within ancient societies; establishing a fundamental conviction that equal opportunity existed for everyone, allowing progress according to each individual's present ability and diligent personal efforts.[2] Harmony was thought to result from establishing or structuring such an 'ordered society' that would then be in accord with that sacred Cosmic Order.[3]

But that ancient accountability and 'take charge' attitude has further eroded during modern times. Many of us have heard the popular refrain that "life is not fair." Some readers may have even expressed that notion sometime during their past. Perhaps life is not fair. Maybe it was never meant to be. We may simply be judging life from a skewed or incorrect perspective. With the knowledge that reincarnation allows all the time throughout eternity to address our faults and perfect our essence, the lessons and trials we encounter during each life should become easier to accept, reducing our suffering and burdens.

Humanity tends to view mortal life with everyone at the same level of development, when in fact we are unique individuals, progressing at different rates from decidedly separate points of reference, all within distinctly different levels of personal growth. We can not expect the same response or result from a kindergarten student that we would anticipate from a corporate executive. Although in some cases, there appears to be little or no distinction when comparing their actions and consequences.

Life is no different. We all have certain finite abilities, reflecting our individually obtained enlightenment level. That potential can either be increased or decreased, depending upon actions committed during each mortal life. Too often we view life as a one-shot chance to succeed, pursue pleasure, gain wealth and material goods, and achieve power and control. And if we have not compromised too many values, or been caught committing too many indiscretions, we may even be rewarded with eternal life in heaven, or suffer in hell if not so lucky.

Luck should have nothing to do with our destiny or fate. Indeed, it is through our own actions that our future is established. We all reach a point in life when we search for deeper meaning. Our perspective either aids or impairs that quest. Evaluation of new thoughts and ideas requires openness and patience, since altering one's beliefs may produce feelings of abandonment and betrayal. New beliefs may conflict with our prior understanding. But take comfort in knowing that new beliefs seldom require total eradication or abandonment of previous ones, often requiring merely a change in perspective.

It may not be possible to classify our deeds within an absolute framework of right or wrong while in the physical world, since so much depends on each individual's present capabilities, and how they perceive and process current thoughts. Those elements combine to determine the true intent of each action, although that does not alter the fact that all occurrences are either Good or Evil under Natural Law.

However, what might be 'right' for an individual presently, may well be 'wrong' for that same person when reevaluated within a future 'expanded' enlightenment level, as gauged through their resultant increase in understanding and wisdom. An individual's comprehensive level always forms the basis of true intent. Unfortunately, much injustice in our world results from humanity's own ignorance. We simply do not understand that something may be wrong, due to the manner in which we interpret and process external stimuli and data. Our present perception and judgment always affects our subsequent actions. As all things undergo change, including our perspective, the ability to perceive between right-or-wrong action becomes clearer.

Regardless, the actual reality of Good and Evil never changes. They are absolute universal constants, the altruism of Natural Law. Evil is always evil, regardless if perceived, identified, or understood by the individual; even when such acts are deemed 'acceptable' within secular laws of society. Although injury, damage, or embarrassment may transpire from such actions, there is no 'sin' in doing wrong, only stagnation and negative karma created by such actions. Sin appears to be a religious concept that apparently does not exist. While such acts may be wrong, requiring future retribution as compensation, they are not sins. Such 'wrongs' are frequently committed out of ignorance, laziness, greed, or temptation, which are often associated with various tests that were intended to be encountered throughout life. Ultimately, karma always compensates for those transgressions, equalizing and atoning for them through implementation of future positive acts.

Failure to learn from life's lessons merely creates the need for future repetitive tests, until correction of those specific deficiencies finally occurs. Conversely, one's enlightenment level is reduced when acts of 'pure evil' are committed. Those continuing to engage in evil actions are regressing (or perhaps progressing, depending on their perspective or intended path) toward perfection of pure evil.

Secular laws are created by humans lacking full enlightenment, and thus are incapable of truly determining what actions and conduct may be most appropriate or 'correct' for society. Because a certain action is considered 'legal' does not infer that such conduct is 'correct' rather than 'wrong.' Society considers the execution of certain convicted criminals as 'legal' in many states. Killing animals within certain guidelines during hunting season is legal. Medical termination of developing human life through on-demand abortion is also legal.

Such lawful 'rights' would seemingly indicate that killing is acceptable and legal, at least when conducted during certain instances, according to human law. Although killing is never acceptable under Natural Law, it is often permitted and even encouraged under certain conditions within secular laws. Justifiable acts of war, self-defense, and judicially sanctioned executions seemingly fall into that category.

Realizing or knowing that things are either Good or Evil does not mean we have gained sufficient enlightenment to reach the point of being able to act in a rigid manner within those absolutes. I submit myself as an example. I know that all killing is evil and wrong. However, I strongly support the death penalty for certain convicted murderers. I am against the liberal practice of abortion-on-demand as a method of contraception. Yet I accept killing in justifiable self-defense and acts of war. While against non-medically-necessary abortions, I support those rare situations where abortion is absolutely necessary to save the mother's life. These are personal 'gray areas' in which we accept or excuse certain conflicted aspects of life within our present belief system. Yet I know killing in any form to be evil and entirely wrong. But I just admitted to exceptions or 'gray areas' within that rigid conviction. However, those 'exemptions' are neither blatant contradictions, nor hypocritical excuses.

Such a seemingly sanctimonious 'explanation' merely proves that I have not yet gained sufficient personal enlightenment, to a level at which my convictions and actions have reached equilibrium with my knowledge and beliefs. Hence, I have not fully developed in those specific areas and have yet to make that transition to where all my actions parallel my convictions.

Full acceptance of any new belief and its application within life requires time, practice, and effort. That starts with an awareness of the need for a new belief, one that supplies answers for life's purpose. That always requires individual commitment and personal effort. Still, I doubt if such growth, as it pertains to my stated convictions toward killing, will be obtained within my present life-span, or perhaps even within my next existence, thereby allowing me to finally obtain that equilibrium between my convictions and knowledge. However, I do envision achieving that enlightenment within some subsequent life, wherein my future actions parallel my convictions and become a retained character trait that carries-over throughout all subsequent lives.

We look for guidance in dealing with these 'gray areas' in life. But there are no true 'gray areas,' only the absolute and universal truths of Good and Evil under Natural Law. But society seeks contradictions, loopholes, excuses, and

117

exceptions in order to justify its actions. To ease the human conscience, humanity accepts actions inconsistent with its obtained knowledge.

Understand that such inconsistency is normal, resulting from differing levels of personal growth accumulated over numerous lifetimes. That growth is obtained by traversing our 'stepping stones' of life, those 'building blocks' of learning, correction, and enlightenment. Such a path is the intended evolution of each soul, its gradual step by step progress toward perfection.

We live in a physical world of what we believe to be reality, but all too often it is merely a mirror of our expectations. Our own actions; those of our neighbors; or even daily mundane life can not disappoint us; only our expectations disappoint. Our unrealistic expectations cloud our perspective and cause suffering. The insightful English novelist and poet, George Eliot (aka Mary Ann Evans, 1819-1880), wrote of disappointing expectations in her 1861 novel, *Silas Marner*, stating, "Nothing is so good as it seems beforehand."[4] Many of us have likely shared similar moments of such disillusionment, due to harboring unrealistic expectations.

Every past, present, or future existence is confined within the physical boundaries of human expectancy. Our expectations within this corporeal realm shape our perceptions and thinking, which in turn influences our behavior. Our expectations condition us to see things as we imagine them, but often simply miss all that surrounds us. We do not comprehend what we view, but merely recognize and record what we choose to see. We look at our watch, but seldom register the present time, realizing that some other past or future time is not currently at hand. We can view the same scene or surroundings, yet see a completely different reality from others viewing that event, depending on our perspective. Hence, the true nature of the world escapes our comprehension, permitting only what we imagine or perhaps 'wish' life could be.

Life then becomes a contradiction, constantly creating internal conflict. Although we may be able to function within that false environment, we can not perform at our best level. As we choose to avoid the present moment, living either in the past or the future, we create opinions, not facts. Those opinions then become our reality, even if they are false.

Believing in something strongly does not alter reality. In olden times, the scientific world believed the world was flat, rationalizing that all other heavenly bodies revolved around that flat Earth, which was located at the center of their perceived universe. Those beliefs, no matter how strongly held, did not alter the reality of our spherical planet revolving around a central sun. Fanatics harbor no doubt that their convictions are equally correct, but belief is not reality.

Nor can 'denial' alter reality. Refusing to acknowledge problems or character deficiencies will not make them disappear. Blaming others for our problems or rejecting accountability for our own actions changes nothing. As we continue to perceive life as a reflection of expectations and faulty perceptions, our 'distortions' become reality, prohibiting necessary changes.

But change can produce temporary problems. Doubts and confusion often result when long held habits and beliefs are suddenly interrupted. As faulty perceptions change, we often lose our 'foundation' or point of reference, producing a sense of loss and confusion. But once the world appears to support and agree with those new perspectives, uncertainty and doubt can quickly dissipate.

From an individual perspective, one tends to view any given environment as the 'norm,' whether it is enslavement, abuse, denigration, or other similar 'controlling' conditions. These demeaning situations are often accepted and thought to be merely the treatment that we deserve. Even when finally removed from those self-defeating influences, victims frequently gravitate toward similar situations or individuals, merely replacing their previous bad environment with another of equal abuse. Some may simply replicate past treatment, actually seeking it out, until they ultimately recognize and eventually alter their incorrect perception. We are doomed to continually repeat self-defeating patterns until we finally embrace and implement the proper perspective on life.

Those not learning from history seem doomed to repeat it. Merely duplicating the same test over and over while refusing to learn from those lessons simply wastes time and opportunity. But that is also the 'beauty' of reincarnation, where tests are allowed to be taken as often as necessary until passing. As faults are identified, corrective measures can then be implemented, permitting those required changes to finally overcome repetitive past cycles. Recognize that our perspective can produce the most secure prison, thus prohibiting any ensuing progress. Only by escaping that self-imposed incarceration can effort then be exerted toward our next trial or life-lesson.

Truth is not always an inherent part of perception. But truth can verify new beliefs based on observed positive outcomes from life's events. Such empirical confirmation leads to knowledge. But faulty perception can impede acquisition of knowledge, since knowledge is always evolving and requires interaction with each progressive 'stepping stone' encountered along our life-path.

Each new discovery or bit of obtained knowledge then leads to further understanding. This process builds upon itself, providing additional wisdom and understanding. That leads to ultimate truth, with truth being its own reward. Do not be swayed by society's current version of the truth. Rather, establish eternal truth by overcoming ignorance and misconceptions.

Society constantly produces fads and gimmicks. Most are insignificant notions professing a 'pop-psychology' mentality, such as the cup being half full, instead of half empty. While optimism is the best attitude with which to experience life, a large dose of realism helps to keep us 'grounded.' The capacity of half a cup, viewed from either perspective, still contains four fluid ounces. Such gimmicks do not change reality.

Accepting that life is developing as it was intended allows lessons and discoveries to occur. As false perceptions are recognized and corrected, a more rewarding and fulfilling life will follow. However, expect to have some 'down days' also, in which irritability, disagreement, and antagonism seem to prevail. Similar to those days when we feel ill of health, our psyche can also experience an occasional 'off day,' which is only normal.

A correct perspective establishes proper priorities, recognizing what is worthwhile in life, while discarding the rest. Timing is everything, since life waits for no one. We can not go back and experience a special moment that passed us by, simply because we did not have time for it while it was first unfolding. Events emerge during periods in life when we are ready and capable of dealing with those occurrences. Interaction with those events is an opportunity for learning.

A skewed perspective often prohibits our learning from those unfolding lesson-events. We may trudge aimlessly through life and continue to miss the importance of all that is around. Life comes only one day at a time. Regretting the past or worrying about the future removes us from living in the present. Accept life as it unfolds, closing doors to the past and ending chapters that have concluded. Do not speculate on future chapters. Read the words that are now within our view, moving us through the present and into the future. Life is an accumulation of events, with no single event representing life's ultimate meaning or purpose, but merely individual learning opportunities from which we can correct and grow. Allow those destined events to present themselves at their proper time and place along our current life-path.

Our past has shaped our present character, while our present actions will shape our future character. We can not change or alter the past, but we can control and modify the present, which shapes our future and our ultimate destiny. We alone control our fate. Perhaps that belief is best demonstrated by the words of poet T. S. Eliot (1888-1965) in his quote: "Time present and time past are both perhaps present in time future, and time future contained in time past."[5] The sum of our past comprises what we are presently, as the present forms our future composition.

Take pause from time to time to assess life, while guarding against becoming trapped in the past. Are we content with the way life is unfolding and developing? Do we have the wisdom to know what is important in life, and what is not? Are we pleased with the aspects and traits that presently comprise our character and how they relate to daily life? Can the things we like about ourselves be identified, along with those aspects we dislike? Can we understand why we do the things we do, and the reason why other acts are left undone? Are we comfortable with our assessment? Socrates (464- 399 BC), the great Greek philosopher, reportedly stated: "The unexamined life is not worth living."[6]

With recognition and regret over past transgressions, along with realization of our still-retained faults, our remaining 'corrections' may seem overwhelming. It can appear to be too much to do within one lifetime, with the resultant frustration becoming self-defeating. But reincarnation provides a glimmer of hope, offering the opportunity for each of us to do our best, while correcting the most deficiencies within our present lifetime and still having unlimited opportunities for additional improvement during some future existence. It is the realization that correction and change always starts with the first step, while always knowing that we have an eternity of additional lifetimes to achieve all those corrective steps.

We are disconnected from our true consciousness while in the physical realm, which can alter our perspective by suppressing and overshadowing those previously nurtured impressions of prior life. The human mind is intended to function in a selective manner, one that essentially determines what is important for retention by our 'permanent' memory, our *Ba*, upon return to the spiritual realm; with less significant data being discarded and forgotten. While in the physical world, there is a finite limit to the amount of stimuli the human mind can endure and comprehend. Poet T. S. Eliot may have perceived such a mortal limitation within his claim: "Human kind cannot bear very much reality."[7] Modern science seems to confirm that belief.

The basic principle of physical existence relates to how we respond to events encountered throughout life. Each mortal life is a successive next step within our evolution towards perfection. That evolution can only occur by experiencing life's lessons, without aid of our past knowledge, so as not to influence our true development by favoring one direction over another, or confusing and overwhelming us with a flood of stimuli. Even with occasional glimpses from past lives, or *déjà vu* occurrences, our perception is so altered while in the physical realm that we dismiss those prior memories. That dismissal is often based on a fear of losing tangible beliefs retained from previous physical existences, even if those beliefs may be incorrect. There is a subconscious attempt to maintain what we perceive as reality, but may merely be our imaginings.

If indeed we chose to come back for further learning and correction, even agreeing to our new life-path trials and lessons, then why does life have to be so hard and cruel? The simple answer is that we learn from the severe and difficult, yet tend to expect the good and easy as the norm. Occasional disruptions within physical life create 'breaks' that allow assessment of our current status, and prompt changes in our perception.

A faulty perspective distorts recognition and understanding. We curse our misfortune, when we should be counting our blessings. A rough past or difficult life can be a gift, providing an abundance of lessons from which to learn, correct, and acquire enlightenment. We may require that level of severity within our present life-path events for certain lessons to finally be recognized and understood, thereby implementing the necessary correction of those flaws.

Only when we accept the challenge of our present lessons can learning and correction transpire. During that period of full enlightenment while between mortal lives within the spiritual realm (when we plan future lessons and trials), it is conceivable that we would freely choose to accept a life-path that would appear to be difficult and challenging. Such a life-path affords abundant opportunities to overcome retained deficiencies that might have eluded prior correction attempts over numerous lifetimes. Such severe lessons focus our attention to assure correction of those deficiencies, breaking the necessity for repetitive lessons during future lives; thereby allowing new trials to be offered in subsequent incarnations for modification of other imperfections.

However our choice in determining subsequent life-paths is limited by our level of achieved enlightenment. Hence, available choices for destined lesson-events are restricted, based on our acquired karma, enlightenment level, and the 'severity' of our retained character deficiencies. Such faults may require concentrated or severe lessons that will finally provoke us to take actions necessary to correct those 'stubborn' flaws. Sometimes those lessons are only available with a 'less than desirable' life-path. But such a challenging life might eliminate the need for additional future 'dreary' existences that essentially repeat the same 'severe' lesson.

Humans are imperfect beings that make mistakes. We would not be undergoing incarnated mortal lives if perfected. Learning from our mistakes creates a more fulfilled life in the future. Performing at our best level minimizes the suffering associated with this on-going learning and correction process, and ultimately reduces future suffering. Learning to laugh at our mistakes may also reduce the severity of those lessons.

Chapter Seven

Choices & Pursuits

With every 'fresh' incarnation, each new life-path presents a multitude of events that require choices to be made. Without aid of our past experiences, it is in our best interest to make correct decisions. With knowledge of the reincarnation process, those choices can be based on the 'larger picture,' rather than on mere superficial desires for instant gratification. Realize that every decision shapes not only our current life, but also carries over into future incarnations. The easy way seldom produces anything of lasting value. The earlier we confront and overcome our difficult trials planned for this life; additional suffering and disappointment can be eliminated from our subsequent lives.

Many in our society claim "they didn't ask to be born." Hence, their implication is that something is owed to them. From what I have been able to verify, no documentation exists as to anyone, past or present, ever 'asking' to be born. At the very least, during that time when each of us experienced our initial and unique embodiment (that instant of creation that produced one's distinct soul or essence), we all started out naked, equal, and neutral from Good or Evil. So why were we born? Why are we here? It is doubtful that life's purpose is the perpetuation of our species. Currently, our world is already burdened with depleting resources and overcrowding. Fewer people would appear to be the better choice, not more.

Perhaps life's purpose is the advancement of civilization. But one can envision a finite point of diminishing return, based on potential consequences from our technological advancements. Humanity might reach a point when machines perform all of our work and thought. Hence, one could argue the possibility of a potential 'species obsolescence' from such technological advances. That is hardly a reason for any of us to be here, or strive for scientific progress.

Rather, I believe that the grand purpose of life is the perfection of our essence. Such a goal is achieved through incremental 'gains' made by each individual over numerous existences. The correction of all deviant behavioral traits then produces a Master Level being. With achievement of widespread universal perfection, harmony and unity could exist throughout the cosmos. Conversely, those seeking perfection in the opposite direction would result in Pure Evil. However, this writing chooses to focus on the perfection of Good.

Frequently the mere act of living can be difficult. Occasionally it can become overwhelming, resulting in individuals abandoning that effort. But anything worth having is also worth the hardship and labor to achieve it. There exist no tricks, secrets, short cuts, or mystical aids such as spells or charms to ease the necessary work and commitment required. No pills, schemes, fads, or instant fixes will achieve the incremental gains necessary to achieve individual perfection.

Each small success puts us ever closer to that perfection. Regardless of our presently obtained level of development, everyone possesses an ability to contribute, correct, and improve. Never give up on life. However small our current progress may be, it will be recognized and rewarded. As incremental progress is achieved within our present capacity, every subsequent life can then build upon all past achievements. Every gain means less hardship in the future.

Elimination of specific 'character deficiencies' starts with the identification of problems and the realization they will remain a part of our life until necessary effort is directed to correct them. As corrections occur, subsequent growth in enlightenment is achieved. To help ease the difficulty associated with such an endeavor, think in small incremental steps, our stepping stones of life. As small 'intermediate' goals are established, based on our present needs, each successful step adds up, encouraging further progress. But undertake only one step at a time, never looking ahead to the next challenge. Master what is at hand, focusing on actions necessary to achieve each intermediate goal, constantly adding to an ever-stronger foundation.

As corrections are made, determination and confidence builds. Rely only on your own efforts to obtain these goals, since lessons are personalized for each individual's needs. That does not exclude outside support, encouragement, and assistance from family and friends. But personal progress is achievable only by each individual, since the required commitment and effort must always come from within.

The potential to cope with life's trials resides in each of us. As we acquire knowledge while overcoming our daily obstacles, we continually add to our present capabilities, thereby further enhancing our future potential. Quoting again from George Eliot: "Our deeds still travel with us from afar, and what we have been makes us what we are,"[1] perhaps defining the true essence of life's inherent building block approach.

Be careful of what you wish for, you might obtain it. Too often it is not what we hoped it would be, needed, or truly wanted. It may lack satisfaction and may actually be detrimental to our real needs. Many false beliefs arise with a short-term approach, wherein instant gratification or personal gain is sought, rather than considering one's long-term needs. No single experience or event defines life, or becomes the meaning of life. Rather, it is the sum of many small steps and individual corrections that eventually add up to real value.

Along the path taken to achieve our present desires, we may encounter something more valuable than what we were initially seeking. Present desires are often merely the 'tip of an iceberg,' with numerous hidden implications. Understand why something is sought. Perhaps it is for fame, wealth, recognition, glory, career esteem, or adulation from others; all the wrong reasons. If we seek acceptance and admiration of others, we become dependent on those opinions to provide our self-worth. That relinquishes one's 'value' to the whims of others, assuring stagnation, failure, and personal frustration.

Focus on what is needed, such as the positive goal of fault correction. Never desire goals based on fears, or things to avoid, which are negative goals. If we fear the occurrence of some event, we typically relinquish control over life. We simply can not control everything. Unexpected events will always occur, disrupting our plans and direction. Be prepared for the unanticipated. But realize that worry never postponed any event, and will not have any positive effect on the future.

As personal pursuits are achieved, incremental progress should be assessed periodically, allowing any necessary adjustments to be made. Ambitious goals should be divided into several smaller finite steps, since large leaps attempted to achieve monumental undertakings are seldom realized, and their resultant failures tend to preclude further attempts.

Traumatic periods and upheavals in our life also provide opportunities to reassess our values, intentions, and direction. Self-assessment and deep analysis may provide new insight into what our present needs, desires, and goals should be. As learning ensues from life's lessons, our intermediate goals and needs often change, requiring periodic adjustments.

Often, goals are not adequately defined or objectives clearly stated. We aim for nebulous commodities, not fully understanding what their obtainment would entail. We may not fully recognize all consequences, ramifications, and effects those achievements might bring. We may desire success, but that means something different to each individual. It may be wealth, fame, marriage, attention from the opposite sex, or any number of other commodities, which can change throughout different periods of life, as maturity and wisdom ensue from lessons learned.

Retirement is a common example that seems to elude many seeking its rewards. Confusion results from a lack of definition and understanding of retirement. During working life, we dream of retirement; that ultimately earned 'life-of-leisure.' Some people even attempt to plan for that occurrence, however inadequately. But it is our personal definition of this goal that requires understanding. Retirement is only a point in time, a transitory threshold from one life style to another, providing a finite break in routines, separating careers from 'special interests.'

Retirement is not a goal unto itself. It involves the end of one routine and the beginning of another. Its reward involves pursuit of personal interests, hobbies, causes, or other similar passions that provide fulfillment. All too often, we do not ponder existence beyond that transitional point, except possibly to focus on certain monetary considerations. That leaves many unprepared for that transition. We incorrectly think of retirement as the final goal, rather than merely the transition point to a new lifestyle. Some view this change in lifestyle as a failure, due to a loss of their prior prestige and power. Then a life of regret and boredom usually results. Most know of someone finally retiring after years of anticipation, only to observe that person waiting in a 'vegetative state' for something to happen.

Boredom, frustration, and feelings of uselessness could emerge from this change, with imminent death sometimes the inevitable result, simply because that individual's goal was not well defined, properly perceived, or adequately planned. Life always requires our active involvement.

Intermediate and long-term goals are often products of our subconscious, which knows what character deficiencies yet remain. That internal 'gauge' helps assure that we are not overwhelmed by the magnitude of our present task to learn, correct, contribute, and grow. Goals are ultimately chosen based upon what we presently value. But that requires recognition of worth, or conversely what might be detrimental, while also having the wisdom to know what is obtainable and what is not, based on our present capabilities.

It is important to set high goals, yet ones that are realistic and obtainable, since achievement spawns additional accomplishments. Goals challenge our inner abilities, while forcing progress and improvement, reinforcing our obtained character traits.

But realism should also be employed. No person suffers more than those who want what they can not have, or strive for unobtainable goals beyond their present level of development. We can not all be rocket scientists, doctors, or world leaders. Yet our children are told that anything is possible, that each can become President of the United States. While many may become presidential candidates, only one will succeed every four years. Realism is essential, with impossibilities and failures vastly more numerous than successes. That does not necessarily imply that humanity is not capable of any and all accomplishments. With patience, over the expanse of time and numerous life spans, all goals are within our grasp.

However, our present enlightenment level may preclude specific goals that are beyond our present capacity. Likewise, we should be content with what has already been obtained, in both material as well as spiritual possessions, thereby avoiding frustration over what has not yet been acquired and achieved. In time, as further enlightenment is gained, all things become possible, including total perfection.

Shoot for the moon, but keep in mind only a small number of people will actually walk the lunar surface within our lifetime. The gifted athlete must realize that only eight out of ten thousand competitors will ever sign a professional sports contract. While we all desire to be the boss, there can ultimately be only one person in charge. Small things add up to great events and accomplishments. Cumulative events spawn growth and enlightenment, but one great event may spoil us, distorting our perception toward future goals. Goals set too high tend to frustrate and demean our present capacity. Likewise, lower set goals fail to challenge or stimulate our present potential. Realistic and balanced goals allow us to grow incrementally in steps or stages, thus allowing any necessary adjustments to be made during the progress. Pursue all goals with vigor and diligence, while avoiding frustration over the seemingly slow pace of progress. Every journey of a thousand miles always starts with that first step. If we allow ourselves to become overwhelmed with the magnitude of such a trip, we will never attempt that initial step.

Never wait for a more appropriate opportunity, or a time when we might be more proficient. Time waits for no one. Participate by engaging in life, while also contributing to society, always performing at your highest obtained level of accomplishment. One never knows when their current effort may shape their entire future, by finally overcoming a long retained fault or deficiency.

Humankind has the tendency to seek the wrong things in life. We hunger for material goods, riches, and control over others, humankind's propensity for greed. But material goods are transient and do not continue into future incarnations. They are not commodities that can be taken with us into the spiritual realm after corporeal death. Worthwhile values such as positive character traits, morals, knowledge, and perfected skills become possessions for all of eternity by transcending corporeal life, remaining with each individual soul through future incarnations.

Sometimes it is with good intentions that material goods are pursued. Parents might desire to spare their children the disappointments and hardships they themselves endured when young. But parents do a great disservice to their offspring by attempting to provide all those things that they were deprived of as a child. The attempt to make life easier and more fulfilling for our children is noble, but it often produces the opposite result. It deprives children of their opportunity to develop a positive work ethic, self-discipline, and intrinsic core values.

That tends to negate a child's ability to formulate and develop attributes of pride, self-reliance, and independence. Those traits must be instilled in all of us, in order to strengthen our resolve during future times of disruption and misfortune. Think beyond any short-term gratification and consider the consequences of such well intended but counterproductive actions.

Focusing on false goals of material possessions and power merely creates a desire for additional accumulation. As that condition escalates, satisfaction is not merely derived from possessing those riches, but also from the desire to obtain those goods. Such a condition prohibits satisfaction with what is presently owned, always desiring ever more.

Desire then becomes the goal, focusing on acquiring something that is not presently owned. That allows the 'anticipation' to become the primary pursuit, rather than the actual attainment of any desired object. Such people then become envious of others who have less, since they still have the potential to acquire many additional possessions. One may eventually obtain everything, but enjoy nothing. Wisdom is achieved when we realize that wealth is merely the measure of those who are content with what they have.

We do not achieve happiness by pursuing it. Happiness is always a by-product, never a primary goal. It is merely a fleeting emotion that will eventually change and dissipate. Contentment is a more realistic and satisfying goal. It can adapt to change and last through transcending periods in life. True contentment is a state of mind. It exists when we are satisfied with our thoughts, actions, and self worth, content with our present life's progress.

Humanity tends to pit one's actions against those of another, creating a climate of competition. Competition can help us to become the best we can be, but not necessarily the 'overall best' when compared with others. The runner who finished in last place may have lost the race, yet set their own 'personal best' performance, a true victory. Winning is not beating others; it is being the best we can be at all times, based upon our present capabilities.

Competition may produce other elements and facets that may not be as rewarding. We tend to treat many of life's events as a competition. We view obstacles in our way as an enemy to defeat. We typically lose when those obstacles resist. We perceive all others as adversaries, to compete against and defeat in order to obtain our desires. We seek power and control over others to gain superiority. Any achievement won at the expense of another will always diminish our own character. One never advances by working against something, but rather by working towards their goals.

Attainment of certain desires often comes with a high price. Be prepared to pay that price, but be sure that goal is worth the cost. The price may be in the form of a decrease in our innate character. No goal is worth compromising our morals, values, ethics, or standards. As we realize that an inappropriate desire is merely transitory and will require future retribution to balance its negative karma, its real price may be more than we are willing to pay. Recognizing the actual usefulness and value of any desired goal will help establish its true worth.

Identify the expected outcome from achieving a desired goal to determine its true value. If worthwhile, attempt its obtainment with dedicated effort, without any hesitation or wavering commitment. Commitment must be at a one hundred percent level, not merely a casual effort undertaken to a certain point, or a haphazard attempt. No half-hearted effort will fully succeed.

Problems arise not only from our inability to commit, but also with the depth of our commitment. We rationalize that we have committed, when in reality we only went so far, only to some finite point. When failure ensues, we blame others, since we can not conceive that it might be our own lack of commitment that was the problem. We choose never to be at fault, all the while oblivious to the larger picture. Think of commitment in terms of an 'on-off' switch. While one may 'throw' a switch ninety-nine percent of the way, the light will not shine until that switch makes full contact, resulting in a completed circuit.

We often hear that marriage is a give-and-take or fifty-fifty proposition. At a fifty-percent commitment level, marriage and any other relationship or endeavor is doomed to fail. Both parties must give nothing short of one hundred percent effort at all times. No half-hearted effort will ever truly succeed. At best, 'occasional' effort will only allow one to 'get by.' But merely 'getting by' relegates one to continually living a shallow life that results only in frustration and stagnation, one without any progress.

The result of stagnation is the continual wasting of opportunities and time, preventing one from experiencing true harmony and enlightenment. Seek more from life. There is always an abundance of worthwhile goals within our reach. Our responsibility is to focus full effort and dedication toward our present duties and life-path lessons. Regardless of our current enlightenment level, living life at our optimum capability will always satisfy our present needs.

No individual ever requires or needs something that is beyond their present ability or obtained capacity. While those commodities may be desired, they are not necessary to fulfill our mission to correct character flaws, contribute to society, and gain enlightenment. Only those who constantly reach beyond their present limits become frustrated and defeated. Likewise, those who never exercise their full potential to reach for higher goals remain stagnant within their currently achieved level of development.

Chapter Eight

Transitional Change & Growth

In the physical world nothing lasts forever. Over time, continents shift, land masses change, mountains and plains erode, and organic matter decays. Physical life is also merely a phase or transition within an ongoing process of emergence and reformation involving ever-changing elements. Life is conceived and nurtured, followed by growth, contribution, and death. From dust unto dust, with this process repeated continually, ever replenishing our physical world. Thus, everything within mortal life is merely transient, always undergoing alteration.

Due to this continuous change, there is no ultimate, single, or permanent reality within the physical world. All things are in a constant state of flux, no matter how imperceptible that change might be. The history of life on Earth has always involved evolution and constant change. Future events occur as a direct result of all actions within both the past and present, as history continually builds upon what has transpired from prior times and events; all creating humanity's stepping stones of progress.

Life is a back and forth process where progress can be made, while occasionally also sliding back into prior bad habits. It is the process of rebirth from life to life, with constant change resulting in growth, stagnation, or even setbacks along the way. Every individual establishes and controls their own timetable for spiritual evolution, through acceptance or rejection of their present life-path trials and lessons encountered in each incarnation. Many personal delays result from stubbornness in confronting those life-path lessons, thereby deferring any correction of retained character flaws and deficiencies to subsequent lives. That wastes time and opportunities wherein progress could have been made.

The concept of reincarnation provides all the time throughout eternity to encounter learning experiences over and over, until one chooses to confront and overcome each retained or recently acquired character defect. That allows each of us the opportunity to learn from our uniquely planned lessons, make corrections, and gain enlightenment. Only when an individual possesses a desire for change, or when they have suffered long enough and feel they can endure no more, will they finally seize the opportunity to reassess their life and confront their present trials.

We constantly attempt to define our place in life, yet find that we are always in a state of flux, undergoing change. We attempt to be many things throughout life, often reinventing different identities at various times, while hiding our true self. We may even attempt to become what we perceive others would like us to be, and may occasionally allow others to temporarily alter our persona. But such defining, changing, expanding, and refining of one's core identity is only helpful when it actually results in correction of faults.

Our personality and characteristics as a teenager become quite different when we reach 30, 45, or 60 years of age. No entity is ever just a single personality. Everyone is comprised of a mix of different functional demeanors and distinct personalities that can readily be recognized during various periods in life. One may be quite dissimilar around their clergy or grandmother, when compared with their uninhibited actions around their intimate lover. That individual remains the same underlying person, but with a combination or mix of dissimilar behaviors, dependent upon which facet is being presented. Normally, only a partial representation of each underlying character composition is displayed during any specific time, with 'lesser demeanors' often masked by one of our more dominant 'core' personalities.

Interaction with our life-path tests and lessons allows our true character to form, revealing our identity. Liberty Hyde Bailey (1858-1954), the widely-acknowledged "Father of American horticulture," believed in learning through direct observation of the common things within our environment; by constantly being involved with and ever partaking of life itself. He is quoted as saying: "It is better to wear out than rust out."[1] Life is meant to be fully experienced if it is to be meaningful and fulfilling.

As personal characteristics develop and change over time, material things encountered throughout life are equally transient. As soon as they are possessed or experienced, their greatest moment of pleasure or gratification is usually over. Likewise, all events and opportunities that are encountered in the physical realm are also temporary. Take advantage of those events or lose their 'timely opportunity' for possible correction and growth associated with those lessons.

Although such moments are transient, if missed or ignored, they will certainly reemerge during some future rebirth. Nothing is permanently lost forever, with everything subjected to some form of continuance, as well as constant change. Life is always at a threshold, balanced on a knife's edge at some finite point representing merely a brief instant in time that separates the past from the future. Since that separation is in such close proximity between yesterday and tomorrow, it is quite easy to drift back and forth between what has been, and what is yet to come, often allowing the present to simply be ignored.

Sometimes the past can look enticing in retrospect. But be mindful to always approach the future with the belief that it can be even better than the past. That the future is developing as intended, providing meaningful life experiences from which to learn. The importance within life emerges from how we interact with our encountered events and life-path trials.

Each unfolding event throughout life is linked with our

present underlying attitudes and attainment level. Present traits have been shaped by residuals from our past. Our present feelings, thoughts, attitudes, and actions not only reflect our current level of enlightenment and character development, but also influence how future events unfold and affect life. Our present life-trials are retained within our subconscious, which were planned as learning opportunities during the review of our most recent 'past-life' prior to our current incarnation. Those lessons influence our feelings and actions toward future events within the present life. We are somehow attracted to those planned occurrences and drawn into their influence as they develop and unfold.

Our only control is over the present, never the past or future. As a known commodity, the perceived security of our past can sometimes form a prison. We may falsely perceive that prison to be a sanctuary, but its true effect is always isolation. As we move away from what we are presently, venturing into the unknown toward what we may become, that isolation can produce feelings of abandonment, even if we are leaving a bad situation or disruptive trait behind. Our mind can simply deny, forget, or distort the pain of those negative experiences, in an attempt to protect itself.

That limits interaction with life while in the present, prohibiting correction and growth. The intent of physical life is to interact with the new encounters that await throughout our present life-path. Without successful interaction with those lessons, we are destined to continually repeat difficult situations and bad relationships until our underlying character deficiencies are recognized and addressed.

Correction of retained deficiencies then reshapes our future actions, attitudes, and outlook, while also expanding our positive opportunities. Future additional lessons and trials would then no longer be required to correct those specific deficiencies, substituting more positive events. Future trials may still address those same traits, perhaps as object lessons from which others might learn, or as further reinforcement, assuring continued 'corrected' behavior until those characteristics are fully mastered and become truly ingrained responses.

It is within the future where our worries, imaginings, desires, and dreams are projected. But such a possible future can be altered or shaped as a direct result of our present deeds and plans. Our present actions and attitudes constantly shape our future, while influencing those life-path lessons yet to come. The importance of a specific life-path trial does not reside solely within its content and details, but also in how we deal with that event.

The present always reflects a new start, a 'clean slate' from which new beginnings can occur. One of the most difficult tasks is to accept change, giving up the old and moving toward the new. Leaving a known commodity and venturing into the unknown can sever our sense of security, regardless of how good or bad that prior situation was. That transition into tomorrow's unknown often produces feelings of apprehension, seclusion, and disruption.

But to achieve progress and growth, we must accept and confront life's challenges, and learn from those lessons in order to grow; or reject change and merely stagnate toward death. The real challenge in dealing with transitions may extend beyond the degree of difficulty associated with those life-lessons and include the ability to recognize when to relinquish the past and move on with life. Any passage from known to unknown creates disruptions. But such transitions are necessary. They create new confidence to attempt further correction of additionally remaining character flaws.

Each event or life-encounter offers its own potential for learning, thereby allowing resultant correction and growth. Taking short cuts or always pursuing the 'easy-path' in life provides limited growth potential or none at all, especially when those life-lessons are simply overlooked. We may attempt to run non-stop toward the future while only going sideways, or avoid or dismiss our life-path trials and learning opportunities by merely racing in circles.

Growth is not merely the learning or acquisition of new virtues, values, or character traits. It also involves eradication of bad habits and traits that have been cultivated over numerous past lifetimes, which carry forward into present life. Some ingrained 'baggage' or flaws may reflect 'demerits' from negative past-life behaviors that continue to be retained within one's present life. That negative karma must be 'repaid' or balanced through some form of compensation with future positive actions, while also correcting its underlying deficiency.

In our rush to live life, we may understate or completely overlook accomplishments that have been learned and mastered within our present life. Such recognition renews our desire and dedication to tackle additional flaws. But we can not accomplish everything at once. Time for rejuvenation and introspection must also be provided, assuring we are proceeding in the right direction. Life's intended 'stepping stone' approach may seem to be a slow and methodical one, but when gauged against all the time throughout eternity, it is merely a single grain in the collective sands of time.

Live life at your full potential, at your highest plane of attainment. An awareness of your current capability, combined with a positive outlook, will overcome most adversity. Make the most of each day by interacting with all developing events, experience them in the present, never confined within the past or projected into the future.

Life-Paths

Physical life confines us to a linear time-based existence, with each day developing into the next, and so on. Every life-event produces an individual step taken separately in sequence, one after the other. Each incremental encounter cither moves us toward our goal, or further from it. Our choices in how we interact with our life-path trials determine each journey's distance, direction, and duration.

Those choices are mainly based on our presently acquired wisdom and enlightenment level derived from all our past encounters. Responses are sometimes dictated by the probable consequences we associate with a chosen action. Our past provides a storehouse of known experiences from which to formulate responses, while predicting their anticipated results based upon prior events. But relying only on the past disrupts present life, creating a non-linear life-path. That situation can then produce life-path events that are out-of-place and distorted.

Reincarnation's step-by-step building process allows the sum of one's prior accomplishments to steadily accumulate toward their ultimate perfection at the Master Level. But present life-path tests must be encountered without aid of our past memory and knowledge, so as not to influence our character development by subconsciously favoring one response over another. That allows our 'learned' cumulative traits to ultimately become intuitively conditioned responses, permanently ingrained within our innate character.

Resistance to Change

As with any 'new' idea, embrace of the reincarnation concept requires altering one's present belief. Such a transition produces a sense of loss and isolation as we distance our selves from prior beliefs and past habits. As life is then experienced after such a transitional change, those feelings of loss and isolation will eventually be dispelled by the comfort derived from the belief in reincarnation.

Humanity tends to equate the past with what they are now experiencing. We continue to imagine that we enjoy our work, relationships, goals, possessions, and our general state of life, only because we were once happy with those commodities. But necessities change over time and present routines may no longer be what is needed, and may have even become detrimental. We may have simply out-grown or learned all we can from those prior associations, settings, material goods, and situations.

Yet we may continue to view those commodities in their 'old light' or previous value, during a period when we once derived benefit and purpose from them, or been truly content with them. We may deceive ourselves with an out-dated perspective. Refusing to recognize that those aspects no longer fulfill our needs keeps us in a state of limbo, unable to move forward or relinquish the past.

Do not deny or rationalize away indications that signal when change is required. There exists an unconscious desire within humanity to resolve conflict, to maintain control over life. That does not imply creating change for change's sake. One making random and wholesale changes may go nowhere, without achieving any progress or growth. Neither can we become merely passive observers in life, severing emotional ties with society and refusing to participate. Time does not stand still. Withdrawal into a cocoon will not stop life; it will merely stagnate and stifle it. The challenge is to manage transitions without disrupting our life-path events, or rush blindly through some ill-conceived life style change.

The security or desperation of one's economic status, especially during later life, may either encourage or preclude their desire to remain in their current situation. It can make one reluctant to give up the known security of attained wealth gained over their lifetime, vainly fighting impending death with fruitless and extraordinary measures, even though that person is no longer learning, progressing, or contributing. Conversely, one's ever-decreasing financial status might inspire certain destitute senior citizens or others in ill health to simply give up on life, no longer putting forth the required effort necessary to alter their deteriorating condition.

We prolong these inner conflicts by seeking and creating excuses that postpone required changes. We may even rationalize that by never exercising our free will choice, we will never be blamed for being 'wrong.' We falsely rationalize that others actually control our fate, since no personal decisions were actually made. That suspends our control over life, absolving us from any responsibility in subsequent outcomes. Such an approach to life only thrusts that individual into becoming a victim of circumstances, a 'puppet' functioning solely at the discretion of others.

Similar to acts of denial or resistance to change, we can often become too comfortable and complacent with our present status. Such a condition can produce a false sense of contentment, negating new life experiences and subsequent learning. Studies seeking to derive wisdom from people that have reached an advanced age have indicated a common regret in life. Those elderly citizens revealed their greatest regret was in not taking more chances during life. They wished they had partaken in additional ventures when younger, by taking measured risks and chances. We may conclude that humanity limits potential opportunities by not sampling the many varied aspects of life. These 'elected' omissions limit the range of experiences from which we base our likes and dislikes, as well as our interests or apathetic tendencies. Taking chances always poses risks, since there are no guarantees in life; but with risks also comes rewards.

We severely limit our ability to make educated and informed choices by refusing to experience life's many facets. Free will choice offers every option in selecting or rejecting any encounter in life, including any subsequent risks they might pose. By logically evaluating the consequences and options, choices become easier. If decisions are not apparent or do not feel comfortable, one may not yet be prepared to interact with those situations. It would then be prudent to delay such interaction until the necessary understanding is acquired to adequately deal with that life-lesson. Life-path trials always require participants to have obtained a level of preparedness equal to its lesson, in order to achieve meaningful results and progress.

143

Throughout life, our greatest asset is our free will choice. Typically, with any given event in life, we have three basic options at our disposal: accept it, change it, or discard it. When an event or association has fulfilled its intent, and all that could be learned has transpired, one must then employ one of those basic options.

Introspection is a necessary step when attempting transitions in life. That involves taking personal 'inventory' to ensure all learning, correction, and growth from an event was achieved. Once a decision is made, let go of the past. Do not dwell on what can not be changed, or what could have been. Proceed with life in the present, without reliving the past. The end of anything is also the beginning of something new. Quoting again from T. S. Eliot: "The end is where we start from."[2] Know that tomorrow always provides a fresh beginning, one without any mistakes.

Physical life

Life is a series of events, experiences, and choices from which we establish our true character composition. That determines our traits, habits, and behavioral characteristics, which form our personal value system. Those developed intuitive and conditioned character responses are retained from one life to the next, unless changed. This ongoing process involves moving away from what we are presently and venturing into the unknown. Such encounters can lead to major life changes, allowing one to move away from their youthful past, while gracefully accepting maturity with all its ensuing challenges and wisdom.

The meaning of life is not discovered in philosophy. Philosophy merely explains a belief system, the mechanics of a given way-of-life. It does not provide a secret plan or map for either success or happiness. Life's meaning is derived from experiencing and interacting with the world, reaping its many benefits. Achievements come from being attentive and alert, acquiring the ability to listen, observe, and learn from involvement with unfolding life. Do not merely view a scene, become a part of it. Allow life's lessons to develop, along with their associated learning, realizing such events are only temporary. Although those events are only momentary, their impact can be permanent when meaningful and life changing, becoming eternal within our memory and character.

Change can occasionally produce an equal or greater level of suffering than what previously existed. Although temporary, such transitional anguish may be a necessary ingredient for our continued progress. Transient distress can be equated with the pain experienced from an operation on one's body, performed in an effort to regain health. Recovery occurs over time. Life changes may be equally painful, requiring correction of chronic character deficiencies. But it is through such difficult and painful change that lasting beneficial results are ultimately produced.

We pass through many transitions during mortal life. Along with feelings of loss, those changes may leave us feeling empty and without direction, even when we are moving forward. Those feelings can restrict us from embracing further changes. *But it is imperative to recognize when the time is right to transition from current situations and implement changes.* Such indications surface or become apparent when we grow tired of our work requirements or daily routine duties. Change is also indicated when things become a 'chore' and we no longer put forth the effort and energy that is expected or required, or when the excitement of being together wanes, or when our feelings associated with an event become false and forced. When we no longer want to continue in such a rut, or endure its suffering, or have learned all that can be derived from such a situation, it is then time for change.

Yet none of those situations suggests abrupt changes or ending relationships. Wholesale changes are rarely the answer. Rather, reassessment of attitudes, needs, and personal goals may merely be required. Perhaps minor adjustments to present situations might be adequate to produce growth. Be aware of your current circumstances and personal passions to establish present priorities. Develop that nebulous ability to know when to hold, and when to let go.

Any transition is an active event that requires work and dedication in order to achieve and implement the desired result. I have a friend who avidly reads inspirational and self-help books. She embraces everything she reads in print, believing that by merely reading about specific character improvements, she immediately and miraculously acquires and implements those specific good traits within her own character composition, retaining them as permanent traits. Thankfully, she does not read serial killer biographies.

Making changes to improve one's character by correcting aberrant behavior is more involved than simply reading books. It requires much more than mere desire, good intentions, or self-analysis. It goes beyond self-help books or attending classes and lectures. Change does not simply happen overnight. It requires individual commitment, desire, discipline, understanding, and action through personal effort. Through focus and effort, changes can become indelibly ingrained as permanent intuitive character responses. But change must always emerge from within, with progress obtained only through personal resolve and dedicated work.

Physical Death

A natural and necessary part of every individual life-path must include its termination through physical death, a transition all mortals must eventually make. Any attempt to alter the inevitable reality of mortality would form an impediment to humankind's ultimate progress. Death is a required passage that initiates the periodic rejuvenation of our temporal vessel or interim body that houses our true essence. Since each life represents a single building block toward growth, all of us will eventually reach a point at which we basically deplete this 'temporary' resource.

Death defines a finite point at which our physical body has become detrimental to any further growth. Death is the mechanism that provides transitional rejuvenation, through subsequent rebirth from a self-perpetuating source of vessels provided by humanity itself. Perhaps youth is not 'wasted on the young' after all, with its ability to provide replacement bodies in the form of babies for unlimited future lives.

A few people harboring a strong religious belief in some type of heaven or hell tend to exhibit a perplexing contradiction. They often profess an extraordinary fear of corporeal death. I am not suggesting it is necessarily wise or healthy to possess a desire or longing for death, since learning experiences can occur throughout all phases of life, with one's greatest lesson opportunity perhaps yet awaiting them during their future 'golden' years of present life.

Rather, it appears that persons harboring such an irrational fear may not possess a true conviction with their religious belief. Certain doubts may possibly exist, either consciously or subconsciously, which could be the cause of their anxiety. That alone should be sufficient reason to reassess or reevaluate one's present beliefs. Above all, such 'personal convictions' or spiritual beliefs should be comfortable ones that provide positive purpose and direction throughout life. Along with our future desires, the potential for what we can become is contained within the sum and substance of the present life being lived, as well as within all the ingrained 'core values' we currently possess.

147

Chapter Nine

Balance & Moderation

Humanity too often values the wrong things. Selfish pursuits appear to be the ambition of many people. Greed and a quest for power, often stemming from envy and a desire to control others, frequently fuel such erroneous objectives. To advance toward our ultimate goal of perfection at the Master Level, a balance is required between human frailties and altruistic behavior. A root cause of much suffering in society results from our inability to achieve that equilibrium, resulting in humanity's seemingly persistent state of turmoil, envy, and aggressiveness.

Humanity, either as individuals or entire nations, often permits bad situations to become catastrophes before finally attempting to solve lingering problems. Hence, imbalances naturally increase by simply letting things go too far, as a result of our inefficient manner of dealing with the many trials encountered throughout mortal life.

Regardless if our problems are social, economic, corporate, environmental, or political, humanity has a tendency to create imbalances by initially doing nothing to address those issues. That inactivity then allows those problems to fester and grow in magnitude. When corrections are ultimately attempted after problems reach epic proportions, society tends to go too far with over-reactive 'solutions.' Such excessive action swings the pendulum from one side (profound neglect), to its opposite extreme (contentious interference), never quite achieving that central equilibrium of true balance.

New problems develop as a result of those extreme

swings, without ever solving the original dilemma. As attempts to correct those new problems are combined with the previous ones, the pendulum again swings toward its opposite extreme, still searching for that elusive solution. Through society's poorly timed actions and ineffective efforts, humanity is constantly 'going past center,' always out of balance. That produces an endless string of inactivity to over-reaction, going from one extreme to another.

Personal life is no different. The tendency exists to jump headlong into society's latest fad that promises to solve all our problems. We freely abandon our most recent 'craze,' becoming enamored with new found hope in the latest 'miracle fix.' Such imbalances tend to produce the workaholic, the sports fanatic, the obnoxious social reformer, the religious zealot, the overly protective doting parent, the habitual worrier, or any number of other such excessive-compulsive behaviors.

Mortal life requires balance as well as focus and effort. It should consist of a blended cross-section or mix of all aspects offered in life, with everything in moderation. Most things in small doses are harmless, while their excess may become lethal. Although free will choice exists for everyone, a certain amount of self-control and discipline always needs to be employed. However, we should not confuse that 'discipline' with conformity or lack of freedom.

A child given complete freedom would likely eat all the candy they wanted, and never go to school, without recognizing the long term health effects, or the harm done to their future adult life as a result of those actions. Some leisure time or small 'treat' may not be detrimental, but their excess could be. A little alcohol may not be harmful, perhaps even beneficial according to some medical evidence, but excessive use always causes problems. By its very nature, freedom also requires moderation. Without moderation, freedom's free will choice can be detrimental.

Living requires us to make choices, but making choices

requires no skill, with bad choices being just as likely as good ones. Anyone can make choices and decisions, but they may not be equipped to make the best selections. The correct or optimal choice requires a certain amount of information and understanding. It is not always possible to make only good or correct choices for a number of reasons, including background data that may be insufficient or faulty. Other choices may simply be foolish, bad, quick, or unwise decisions.

There are possibly better methods in which to organize groups of people than our present system of civilized society. We continually attempt to manipulate our culture into one of perfection, constantly tinkering with superficial changes in order to achieve utopia. Although perfection of our character composition through attainment of the Master Level is our ultimate goal, perfection within the physical world may not necessarily be desirable. Such attainment may even preclude what may be best for humanity.

A perfect community or idyllic society may be counterproductive to humanity's progress. Such a perfect society would negate events that provide necessary tests or trials for learning along our life-path, eliminating those opportunities for individual correction of deficiencies that could lead to growth. Attainment of societal perfection would create an exquisite governmental environment, but one inhabited and dispensed by imperfect people.

Such social perfection could diminish humankind's ability to achieve correction and growth. The creation of communal perfection might also prohibit innovations or inventions intended to aid humanity, by removing the need for such experimentation and invention. It is humanity's imperfections that supply the intent and incentive necessary to expend effort and resources to pursue solutions and cures, accompanied by the design and production of those helpful aids and corrective innovations that eventually benefit society.

It is in our 'imperfect' physical world where needs arise that require innovative solutions that challenge our abilities, forcing ever-higher achievements. Thus, inherent human imperfections supply the necessity and motive to undertake those corrections, leading to additional progress.

Humanity can learn valuable lessons from the vast universe surrounding us. Our cosmos constantly displays incredible balance, even with its chaos. Evil, along with Good, may even provide the cohesiveness and integrity to the fabric of our universe, whatever that substance may be that surrounds and contains its outer boundaries at the extreme edges of space. Perhaps such a fabric or commodity separates our tangible world from the absolute nothingness beyond. That boundary may represent the barrier separating realities that apparently exist between the physical and spiritual worlds. Perhaps it is the commingling of both Good and Evil that balances karma within the universe. Evil may occasionally provide some essential trials and tests from which learning might occur, thus promoting resultant Good. Our universe seems to provide a similar 'balanced mix' to all life-events, while also allowing free will choice within our responses to each of those occurrences. That permits individual pursuit toward perfection of either Good or Evil, depending upon personal preference.

While perfection within the spiritual realm may be achievable, distortions and imbalances associated with our physical senses and emotions essentially preclude similar perfection while in the material world. Emotions can alter or influence interactions with encountered events in the physical domain, a situation that does not exist within the spiritual realm.

A truly spiritual entity would know that physical life was developing according to the timetable and pace of their own choosing. While in spirit form, we do not possess empathy or other similar physical emotions, since the grand scheme of life is fully understood. It is the realization that no one is irreparably injured or permanently 'dies' as a result of any lessons encountered during mortal life. Such trials are merely learning events from which beneficial correction may result. Within the spiritual realm, love becomes the dominant emotion defining our interaction with others, in a manner similar to its function while in the material world.

During mortal existence, our emotions and physical senses may trigger recognition of unfolding pre-planned life-path lessons intended for learning. Such recognition can then focus our attention and efforts on addressing those current lessons, perhaps prompting their ultimate correction. Similar trials would then no longer be necessary, saving time and effort. Our responses to life-path occurrences require a balance between caution and curiosity, but the desired outcomes must not be used to justify any adverse behavior during such encounters.

Consider humanity's seemingly just and well-intentioned fervor in promoting its different religious beliefs. Throughout history, documentation of man's inhumanity toward fellow man is prevalent; all in the name of religious zeal that was intended to benefit humanity. The Crusades, the Inquisition, the Salem 'witch trials,' and the Spanish colonization of the Americas, along with modern acts by Islamic extremists, all showcase some of humankind's worst atrocities. Yet all were committed, or are still being carried out, in the name of 'religious causes,' although certainly without humanitarian intentions or means toward that end.

Balance always suffers when well-intentioned zealots become fanatical. The extreme methods employed to achieve their goals simply undermined any intended Good originally sought. Focusing energy on a single fixation can create imbalances in life and cause alienation from others. It also creates dependency, as we become reliant on some new 'fix' to solve our problems or 'save' us. That negates the ability to gauge between Good and Evil acts.

There exists a finite balance in nature where

independence is tempered with mutual reliance, allowing a balanced symbiotic relationship. Such natural balances include plants giving off oxygen that is used by humans to produce carbon dioxide, which in turn nourishes those plants. This balanced state of interdependency is always on display throughout nature.

Similar balance must also apply to society as a whole. Distinct or segmented factions that focus only on a singular mission will never solve the ills of society. Those groups lack balance necessary for correction. One can not be for social reform by being opposed to the rights of other groups. Championed ideals never succeed when they are at odds with other causes, and consistently devote much of their efforts toward defeating perceived 'opponents,' rather than furthering their own group's objective or goal.

Conversely, harboring passion for a specific cause should not be considered as being against another objective. Motives behind a specific cause need not be counter to another one. As an example, support of animal rights does not mean that one is against the environment, jobs, child welfare, or any number of other concerns. It usually means the opposite, reflecting a belief that all life and rights are interconnected pieces of the same puzzle that fit together when in balance. Support in one area need not be mutually exclusive of other causes.

Gains resulting from any single-focus pursuit are often only 'stop-gap' approaches, merely temporary measures without lasting results. Change and subsequent correction must start within each individual, the smallest and most basic element of any society. Once we ultimately become 'suitably' tolerant, full acceptance will inevitably follow, with societal conflicts and problems eventually diminishing and perhaps dissipating entirely over time. Being for something while standing against another cause will never end injustice. Hate never defeats inequities; it only fosters further hatred and intolerance. Balance in humanity's thinking, attitudes, and actions is the only hope for lasting correction of society's ills. But there are also limits to certain 'good' characteristics, since some traits can be taken to extremes. One example of excessive good intention is 'tolerance.' Too much tolerance can allow or permit evil or other undesirable traits to proliferate. Non-judgmental tolerance permits the expansion of liberal 'idealism' within a society, allowing acceptance of actions that should actually be deemed unacceptable. Just as 'discriminating taste' is a desirable attribute, discrimination in free will choice can also be good, allowing humans to discriminate or judge whether certain actions within our culture are proper and correct, or if they are misguided and ultimately harmful.

Aspects of personal life and those of select groups do not exist in a vacuum; they affect all of society. Individual tolerance diminishes when viewed against the whole. Permissive or selfish responses to life's 'questionable' occurrences can undermine the rights of others, and disrupt the intended balance within the universe. Underlying flaws within any culture will always evade correction if societal changes only consist of passing more laws, restricting or declaring new rights, adding police enforcement, or enacting other similar secular 'fixes.' Too often those attempted corrections merely add to the magnitude of humanity's current cultural problems.

Societal laws do not correct aberrant behavior. Such laws merely provide a standard that is used in policing actions while we are being watched; offering only limited protection and minimal oversight. When that deterrent is absent or circumvented, it is in our human nature to attempt to get away with what one believes they can. It is ultimately up to each individual to modify their own behavior, by correcting retained deficiencies so society's monitoring efforts are unnecessary. That starts with application of the basic values of Good over Evil, or actions that are right rather than wrong. Humanity's organized religions and secular laws are only basic starting points that merely help define such 'limits' upon society's conduct, while also encouraging positive behavior. Personal efforts leading to correction and ultimate balance can often affect other community members by becoming an example of success, supplying balance for an improved and peaceful society. Only with permanent correction of individual faults will societal problems eventually diminish. With understanding of our intricate purpose and interconnectivity throughout the universe, each new building block resulting from individual correction and personal growth adds to that cosmic balance.

Once humanity corrects its most basic deficiencies, the larger and more complex cultural injustices can then be addressed and overcome permanently. Such solutions must be built upon basic values, commencing with an understanding of a minimal level of 'acceptable' behavior, based on defined values and morality. But the creation and implementation of such a community would seemingly require the complete alteration and major restructuring of our present culture.

Presently, such a massive change may not be possible, due not only to its magnitude, but also the resulting imbalance such an extreme 'pendulum swing' might produce; a rather ironic reason for postponing such change. Perhaps a future massive natural disaster or economic upheaval might provide better timing, or a more appropriate opportunity, for such implementation, which is also a rather somber commentary on the state of our present society.

A solid foundation built upon basic values and decency must underlie any reform. All other approaches would be similar to building the roof of a house before its footings and walls were erected. While a leaking roof is repairable, no lasting or useful outcome can be obtained when the foundation is faulty or absent. Attempts to grasp the grand scheme of life reveals the vast importance of individual correction, one building block at a time. Such awareness, with its resulting correction and progress, can not be legislated, ordered, or decreed into existence by any society. *There is no single greatest moment or aspect of physical life that defines each incarnation.* All of life's events are equally important in providing learning experiences. Life comprises a varied mix of constant stimuli and events for individual interaction. Balancing that mix provides focus, motivation, purpose, and variety to mortal life. Each physical existence will always produce a generous amount of successes that are intermixed with failures. But those individual problems that might arise are actually quite minor when viewed against the grand scheme of eternal life.

Progress will always ensue when balance and discipline is present in life. Such balance can be achieved through diet, exercise, family, introspection, friends, work, hobbies, and moderation within every aspect of life. Our body and mind are then in unison with our spirit, which can then provide adequate resolve and the discipline necessary to maintain our required balance.

Balance can even become a component of our perspective. We continue habits without realizing those actions are subconsciously ingrained, moving ever further from equilibrium. We do not stop and question our present situation, but merely rely on the prior knowledge that our current path was once what we wanted during some previous time period. When our present comfort level is disrupted, we often react by attempting to replace what has been altered or lost by substituting one 'pacifier' with another.

But balance must always be considered. If prior equilibrium was not present before some new disruption emerged, regaining or maintaining one's past status by substituting a 'replacement' will not create balance where none had previously existed. However, we can seize the opportunity that emerges during those times of disruption, and use their 'lessons' to recognize the need to create true balance through personal assessment and subsequent change.

When dealing with disruptive periods in our life, another approach includes replacing a single 'lost' habit or commodity with multiple different 'replacements,' or conversely substituting several 'minor' passions with one 'primary' interest. This approach may even reveal a new major pursuit or interest, broadening our experience and perspective on life. The Greek orator Protagoras (*c*.481-411 BC) stated: "Man is the measure of all things."[1] It is through such a diverse approach that lasting balance can be achieved and maintained. Varied interests expand both insight and choices, exposing us to a greater cross-section of physical life. Our innate character becomes well rounded and balanced from numerous diverse interests and pursuits.

Balance can also be achieved through the acquisition of knowledge. Understanding how things work and interact can provide greater insight as to why events happen and how everything is ultimately connected. That comprehension may even help to explain why we partake in some of life's 'extremes.' We permit internal struggles, creating an ambivalent love/hate relationship. Outwardly, we are vain and self-centered, yet deep down dislike many personal aspects of our own character. Is anyone ever totally satisfied with their intellect, social status, appearance, body image, wealth, or some other similar personal aspect?

It is through our inquisitive nature that knowledge and wisdom are acquired, which provides us with the ability to discern when life may be spiraling out of balance. Wisdom always prevails over pure intellect. Wisdom is the application of knowledge, not merely the accumulation of data, theories, and formulations. Education is not necessarily related to wisdom. One may possess the superior intellect to lead, but not know where they are going. Wisdom is an all encompassing characteristic, allowing distinction between justice and injustice, or right from wrong. It 'senses' the proper course of action or correct direction to follow. Wisdom professes action rather than inaction or reaction, while allowing the contemplative individual their ability to either refrain or interact. In a world where a barrage of stimuli constantly bombards us, it is more important to be able to engage with developing events, rather than merely react to them.

An excess of anything, such as pain or pleasure, or denial or indulgence, only creates further imbalances in life. Most behavioral extremes, such as phobias and aberrant actions, originate from fear. Such an emotional response is not necessarily physical fear, but rather a fear of the unknown. We worry about what might happen, or what our future might bring. Humanity possesses a need-to-know compulsion, yearning to understand why things happen, and how things function. But apprehension surfaces when those answers are not forthcoming. We end up living on the edge, afraid of losing what we already have, regardless of how little that might be; yet remain fearful of moving into the future with its many unknowns.

Fear or shame is often at the root of society's aberrant behavior, fueled by insecurities. Fear always interferes with balance, diffusing life's focus and distorting perspective and judgment. We then react rather than cooperate with unfolding events. But choices are seldom black or white, but usually something in-between. Awareness of the reincarnation process permits facts and data to be evaluated for their long-term consequences within the larger picture, rather than merely their short-term impact. As one obtains additional knowledge approaching perfection, those 'gray areas' will disappear, allowing an unfailing perception of right and wrong.

However, such an enlightened state appears beyond reach for much of humanity, as learning and correction is postponed while we make numerous mistakes along the way. But with each obtained incremental bit of progress, those 'gray areas' will be reduced, resulting in ever-increasing clarity and an accompanying ability to make truly informed decisions in the future.

Deficiencies are not overcome by merely rationalizing them away or fighting them, and certainly not by embracing them. Correction of such character flaws requires both physical and mental effort, along with introspection to discover their basis. At our soul's origin of its first birth, we were all born 'neutral,' devoid of either Good or Evil traits. Only the potential existed for acquisition of negative traits or phobias, as well as more positive attributes. Present aberrant characteristics were acquired along the way, either from some past life, or during one's current incarnation. Such flawed traits will also carry-over into future lives, until they are confronted and corrected by each individual. Many deficiencies are overcome by replacing them with acquired positive traits, through acquisition and application of knowledge and understanding.

It is easy to lose sight of what is important in life, as society provides an endless array of appealing distractions. Balance allows pursuit of multiple interests while still maintaining focus. No individual is just one thing. A murderer is still someone's son or daughter. A teacher is also a husband or wife, while an executive is also a parent. Every one is more than merely a title within their chosen profession, and does not lose all worth once that title is gone. However, some become totally immersed within their profession, enamored with their personal success.

Such an extreme concentration of effort usually occurs at the expense of all else around, including exclusion of family, friends, values, and most personal responsibilities. Many of us have observed or known people who are highly intelligent, schooled within a narrow professional discipline. While they may be experts in their narrow field of study, they are typically incapable of functioning within the vast majority of remaining life. Outside of their narrow scope of vision and specific expertise, they often appear ignorant and out-of-touch with normal life, devoid of any common sense.

There is nothing wrong with passion devoted to a specific field of endeavor, or with some dominant character trait, as long as that concentration does not control that person. If a single aspect dominates one's focus, imbalances occur, producing compulsive behavior. That eventually forms a trap, usurping one's effort and attention at the exclusion of all else. Such a person will often experience fear, disillusionment, and a sense of displacement as they withdraw further from ordinary life.

Such paranoid behavior need not occur. Humankind possesses a natural tendency to function within a balanced zone of existence, one situated between denial and excess. That 'middle-zone' of balance is where physical health and contentment reside. But that region is uniquely different for each individual. As correction and growth occurs, our focal-center may also shift as enlightenment increases.

A focused, well-adjusted, and informed individual, one capable of coping and interacting with mortal life, is equipped with the required balance to recognize their present weaknesses and strengths. That realization provides the necessary motivation to confront and correct remaining character faults. Such a balanced approach to developing life assures success in all things attempted. To again quote George Eliot: "Our deeds determine us, as much as we determine our deeds."[2]

All of us are presently the sum of our past and present life experiences and how we handled those encounters. That cumulative composition helps determine how we will deal with future occurrences, as those events become potential building blocks, or our stepping stones of life. Take comfort in recognizing that all the time in eternity awaits us to accomplish any remaining character corrections.

Consider negative traits and habits as 'voids' that must be filled with positive characteristics. Cold is merely the absence of heat. By introducing a heat source, the cold is replaced with warmth. Individual 'voids' or character deficiencies often persist merely because they remain undetected, overlooked, or simply avoided due to our continuing unenlightened state.

Plan for the future, but never let it obscure or overshadow the present. The ant and grasshopper fable demonstrates the common sense wisdom of planning ahead and working toward the future as a necessary aspect of physical life, but not its sole purpose. We learn from the past, while living in the present, as we plan and prepare for the future, but always within a finite balance between those three phases of existence. Follow your cumulative inherent instincts, your 'gut-feelings,' allowing them to guide you toward your desired goal, while always maintaining life's required balance.

Chapter Ten

Responsibilities & Duties

No equality exists among humankind. That statement has no bearing on race, ethnic origin, gender, religious belief, sexual preference, wealth, intellect, or social status. Quite simply, the world is comprised of different mortals existing at distinct levels of individual progress and spiritual enlightenment, which has resulted from choices made by each person and their self-created timetable toward personal learning, correction, and growth. The world always reflects this mix of variously developed individuals, each engaged in their ultimate pursuit toward the perfection of Good, or their chosen path of regression toward the perfection of Evil if so inclined. Such apparent disparity merely reflects each individual entity undergoing their unique and personal timetable of development, which they chose for their own character evolution.

There was only one moment when all of humanity was essentially equal in status. That was at one's initial creation of consciousness, when every soul started from a neutral point, devoid of both aberrant as well as positive character traits, with a clean slate. Since then, all of us have undergone learning trials or experiences that have changed or altered that initially neutral status, either positively or negatively, to encompass the essence of what we are presently.

But such a journey has spanned many past lives, including one's present life; all ultimately formulating each individual's unique character traits they currently possess. The only other time equality will be achieved is with the attainment of the Master Level, when the perfection of either

Good or Evil is realized.

By categorizing stereotypical groups, nationalities, races, or certain creeds as being confined within a common perceived sameness, humanity discounts the uniqueness of each distinct individual within those broad classifications. No one is just one thing. By elevating or demoting people to some arbitrary norm or grouping, the accomplished Black is downgraded below the level of the struggling White, while the impoverished Jewish worker is upgraded above the obtained level of the successful Hispanic. People are individuals, and should not be relegated to mere categories or groups. Humanity must learn to view people as separate and distinct entities, recognizing those working at their fullest potential, however great or small that level might be.

Since we all initially started as 'neutral vessels' able to be molded into whatever direction or outcome we choose, the capability to determine our own character development is universal. That means each of us must ultimately encounter, learn, and overcome essentially the same basic lessons and trials sometime during our many incarnations. Avoid bemoaning any perceived misfortune as something 'bad' that only happens to us. Each individual has either already endured, or will experience, similar trials and lessons at some future time. Since we encounter those lessons based upon our own chosen timetable of development, those experiences do not occur in any particular sequence or pattern. Rather, they occur randomly when each individual is 'ready' for such encounters. There is no set order or schedule that mandates when lessons, or their subsequent corrections, must occur. We simply develop in our own way, without following any fixed plan.

It is believed that one's spiritual development is somehow intrinsically and inexplicably linked with some greater collective consciousness within the universe. That link may also be mysteriously connected with the Creator, making each of us a part of that Great Source, all intertwined

164

as intended. Conversely, it would appear that the development of our physical vessel (our body) is dependent upon the natural forces of evolution and mutation. But other forces are likely also involved. Perhaps biological and anthropological changes result more from some 'need' to provide additional or expanded physical capabilities to 'developing' humans, as increasingly enlightened souls require such newly 'enhanced' abilities to ultimately achieve their objectives.

Life does not consist of what the world has to offer us. Rather, life's meaning unfolds from what we can contribute to the universe, and how we interact with others while within this physical realm. Do not seek fulfillment from the world, but rather from within. Satisfaction can be derived from the smallest accomplishments. Likewise, it is important to accept and acknowledge the unique input and contributions made by other individuals, based on their present level of abilities, regardless of how small those contributions might be.

Always accept responsibility for your actions, as well as your life-path situations. Since we all possess free will choice, we are always in control. Do not 'curse' encountered suffering, or abstain from certain distasteful situations; they provide valuable learning opportunities. We must continually seek to expand personal horizons and explore new avenues, but only those within our present abilities. Nothing dissuades progress as much as failures caused by attempting goals that are too lofty. Set your sights high, but remain grounded in optimistic realism, always aware of your present abilities and limitations.

Today's slogan 'be anything you can dream' is a misleading and perhaps dangerous belief or concept. It may instill a false sense of one's current ability, while also influencing their choice in pursuing a specific but presently unobtainable goal, thereby subjecting that individual to needless failure. Those failures could negate additional attempts by such dejected individuals, ultimately deterring them from attempting even the simplest correction, thereby prohibiting any personal progress. Believing in one's self is only a single element necessary in obtaining goals. Any desired commodity also requires hard work, determination, discipline, and perseverance for its achievement. Even with full application of those elements, one may still fall short of their mark; but do not despair. Although we can not all be brain surgeons or rocket scientists, the reincarnation process provides all the time throughout eternity that is necessary to eventually accomplish all our desired goals.

An accurate assessment of our present capabilities must be considered when establishing personal endeavors and directions. Defining and planning our approach to life also requires a realistic perspective to identify certain goals that may presently be out of reach. That does not imply such goals are forever inaccessible. Those lofty objectives could eventually become obtainable in the future, after further individual learning, correction, and growth has been achieved. Just as we progress in small steps, we must learn to build upon incremental achievements. While merely being 'average' in a specific discipline during this lifetime, we can become 'accomplished' in that same endeavor within some subsequent life. Remember that anything worth having is worth working for. Strive for that obtainment.

Equal opportunity does not insure equality. Individual qualifications are an essential ingredient in obtaining a job, just as one's attained level of enlightenment is an integral element in determining what life-path opportunities can be included during future incarnations. Thus, equality's only role in society must be in affording all humanity the same fundamental rights, basic privileges, equivalent challenges, and comparable learning opportunities. But how each individual utilizes that 'generalized' equality depends on their uniquely achieved abilities and character development.

Equality is merely the uniform dispensation of fairness. But it requires each individual to be accountable for supplying the effort and focus necessary to derive benefit from their chosen life-path opportunities. That fairness allows 'developing' individuals to progress, and more 'accomplished' ones to excel, extracting each individual's full potential from their own unique level of personal attainment. Such an 'equal opportunity approach' allows contribution from all levels of society, while acknowledging and encouraging individual achievement.

We create the bends and forks along our own unique life-path. Dare to evaluate routes not previously traversed. Our future is not fixed, only our destined learning events are set. We decide our future while in the present, as a result of our free will choice of attitudes and deeds. While predestined events may be scheduled to occur sometime in our future, our interaction with them and their subsequent outcome can not be determined until the time of actual encounter.

Although such lessons are destined to occur, their ultimate reality transpires only from our involvement with those events. The future does not just happen, it is also formed by our present collective efforts and deeds during this life. What we are currently, inclusive of past mistakes and character deficiencies, can be transformed sometime in the future by our efforts in the present, creating a different and better character composition and destiny. It is never too late to alter our path, since all the time in eternity yet awaits our continuing ultimate development.

It is through one's own efforts that correction and progress occurs. Accomplishments in life were never intended to come easily. But never be afraid to fail from such attempts, it is a 'rite-of-passage,' and another element of learning and growth. Sadly, perhaps failure seems to be one of the best ways in which to learn. Painful lessons resulting from failure seemingly create a greater impression on our life, rather than encounters involving more pleasant experiences. But any attained success always requires sacrifice and effort. Progress demands contribution at whatever level we are capable of providing. Mere talk and good intentions only lead to inaction, resulting in postponement and stagnation, a personal form of character and moral bankruptcy.

Tangible contributions result from the impact of our attitudes and actions, which include setting positive examples while harboring optimistic thoughts. Further contributions can be realized by advancing knowledge and understanding whenever possible. And finally, eternal contributions will always occur from the indelible consequences coming from our efforts to improve the tangible world, regardless of how small those individual labors might seem.

All contributions are gifts to our current and future world, the world from which we will later reap the destined benefits of those prior contributions, upon each successive incarnation or return back to this planet. Be aware that each of us can make a difference by the examples we set, and our positive deeds performed. Not the least is the correction of individual character deficiencies. That small contribution of 'self-correction' creates positive influences everywhere, through our unique bond or interconnection with the universe.

Less gifted individuals with 'limited' potential, as gauged by their present development, achieve far greater contributions for the universe and their personal advancement when they function at their maximum present potential, as compared to those that are more capable but operate at only a fraction of their true capacity. The universe expects and demands greater contributions from those having achieved higher enlightenment and expanded capabilities than those with lesser attainment. We have all admired the accomplishments of a handicapped individual competing in the Special Olympics, and scorned a sub-par performance by a professional athlete, even though the 'pro' could easily defeat the Special Olympian. What more can be expected than one hundred percent output from any individual, as based upon their present capability and potential?

By expecting some arbitrary universal achievement level,

one reflecting a uniform measure of output from everyone, society frustrates the unachieved and fails to challenge the more accomplished. The desire for some arbitrary 'performance equality' from every person creates expectations of the impossible from the unenlightened, while accepting less from the gifted.

Humanity's attempt to solve such a performance-disparity often starts with inactivity and denial, followed by over reaction. It seems that society has now found an easy way to eliminate failure and mediocre performance by simply lowering the standards defining 'acceptable' levels, thereby redefining the meaning of success itself. Such a shortsighted solution fails to instill responsibility either in the individual or society as a whole, resulting only in stagnation.

Humanity seems to have a propensity for such denial. We deny that problems exist, or that an individual might have a character deficiency or negative trait. We make excuses for all of society's anomalous actions. We compare one evil against another evil, rationalizing that the lesser offensive trait is therefore acceptable. We often blame our life-situation, our environment and upbringing, or the 'whole of society' as root-causes for all deviant actions. We 'label' problems in an attempt to escape any blame being placed on those committing such infractions. We produce the 'inner-city' criminal and the 'misguided' juvenile delinquent, while labeling alcoholism a 'disease,' or blaming the 'system' for failing the student. Nothing is apparently ever our fault. Such denial falsely implies that we are not accountable for our own actions, forever exchanging personal responsibility for some dubious 'treatment' program.

Perhaps incompetence prevents such an individual from recognizing their own deficiencies, especially when they deny their own culpability due to arrogance or over-confidence. Such a condition can become self-perpetuating, nurtured by a lack of feedback, or incidental input that is incorrectly interpreted as positive reinforcement. Those individuals may lack enlightenment to recognize their own deficiencies and errors, which may be clouded by their extremely high self-opinion, one that is usually wholly unwarranted.

Society even provides rewards for our own mistakes by declaring that we are all 'victims,' awarding us monetary compensation for being a casualty of our own actions. We seem to live by a new creed that no mistake should go unrewarded. We further demand that our elected officials provide instant solutions to humanity's complex problems. Such a belief implies that productive people of society deserve less, while the non-productive should be rewarded with equal or greater prosperity without any worthwhile contribution; essentially a redistribution of wealth.

Such popular theories may be based more on envy rather than on fairness or justice. We may simply be expecting too much from society's governance. Humanity must realize that no one is entitled to anything, other than what has been earned by each individual. It appears that society's present perspective requires change, one that replaces false 'political correctness' with accountability and a sense of duty. The absence of individual responsibility only encourages conflict, with chaos and anarchy as the result. To achieve harmony, everyone must follow minimally established protocols. Such rules, codes, and laws provide the ordered structure and balance within society, while encouraging every individual to become responsible for their own actions.

Perhaps similar regulations transcend our physical world, with Natural Law promoting truth and harmony throughout the universe. Yet human laws lack the consistency and fairness of Natural Law by constantly undergoing change, thus failing to embrace the concept of 'absolutes.' Hence, 'gray areas' are invented to distort the ultimate truth, which is always an 'absolute.'

Our judicial climate, indeed our entire judicial system, has abandoned its pursuit of truth for mere expediency and procedural 'correctness.' Apparently it is now immaterial if a defendant is guilty or innocent. Rather, importance is focused on proper procedural policy and protocol, not true justice. Fairness and accountability has become its victim, replacing truth with image and decorum. Through legal jargon and manipulation of loopholes, the contrived self-interests of judges, lawyers, and even juries can prevail over guilt or innocence, at the expense of justice.

Laws then become counterproductive to the truth, which is abandoned in favor of concocted rights that have spiraled out of control. For the preservation of justice and our court system, society needs to reestablish a version of legal proceedings reflective of Solomon's wisdom. Otherwise, fairness and truth will eventually vanish from our courts and society as a whole.

When unfairness is encountered, we often respond in an aggressive way. But when we use the negatives of hatred and revenge to attack others, they typically turn inward, hurting only ourselves. Most of life's minor aggravations occur from the discourtesy and thoughtlessness of others, not deliberate malice. Retaliation merely increases the level of danger and expands the negatives within such situations, resulting in counterproductive actions that accomplish nothing.

All correctable problems within a society are those created by people. The remaining 'non-correctable' problems are natural forces from which trials and lessons emerge. Until one accepts responsibility for their own actions, rather than asserting such problems are never their fault, personal assessment, correction, and growth can not occur.

It seems to be in vogue for humanity to declare that they carry baggage from a dysfunctional family background. That they were deprived or 'wronged' in some way during adolescence, and thus were victims of inept parenting or other damaging influences. Hence, others are to blame for all their problems. Author John Bradshaw claimed that ninety six percent of us came from such dysfunctional homes, resulting in all kinds of addictions and unhealthy relationships, thus producing the resultant "poor inner-child."[1] Parents are used as scapegoats, often crediting them as being the root cause of our later problems. However, since this 'research' has now deemed that nearly all of us developed within some sort of 'dysfunctional environment,' such an upbringing thus becomes the norm, not the exception.

Using that logic, there is no validity for blaming a difficult background for one's present problems or failures. Since most of us were supposedly nurtured in such an environment, it simply does not account for all the other 'dysfunctional' children that coped with their similar upbringings, yet were able to eventually contribute in positive ways through acceptance of personal responsibility and hard work. It also diminishes the efforts by their 'accused' parents who likely had their own faults and perhaps also raised by parents that had their set of problems. I believe that most parents try to provide their best effort and judgment in raising their children, within their own limited abilities and attained level of development. Since parents are only human, disparities will continue to exist, and mistakes will invariably be made.

Such a view is not meant to minimize the small minority of children that actually endured abusive, neglected, or victimized backgrounds. Their latent wounds from numerous forms of abuse may require assistance from professionals in order to overcome such physical and mental trauma. Those ordeals and scars are real, and pose a major trial to surmount throughout physical life. But many have risen above their past to become truly exemplary role models in society, overcoming obstacles and trials through determination and inner-strength, often irrespective of extraneous help. Such an accomplishment will surely result in increased wisdom and enlightenment. But remaining stagnant and simply accepting 'victim status' will never result in meaningful progress.

Refrain from becoming another 'victim of society,' wherein others are to blame for all our problems, especially inept parenting. Most of us have experienced dysfunctional families in some fashion, but do not allow that to become an excuse for failure. Our culture is obsessed with blaming others for our problems. Dr. Sigmund Freud proposed that the origin of every adversity actually lies within our unconscious, where our thoughts, fantasies, memories, and dreams exist. He further believed that the solution to such problems would be found in the realization and acceptance of those past experiences and their influence over our present life.

But there is no single attribute more important in initiating correction and growth than the acceptance of personal responsibility for our own actions. No excuses, extraneous blame, or focus elsewhere can be allowed. All required correction must start with an awareness and understanding that every character deficiency is fully within our control. If we reject accountability for our actions by blaming external sources for our problems and failures, then exposure and correction of those flaws will simply never commence.

But we live in a society obsessed with condemnation, assigning blame to inanimate objects as being the underlying cause for all the defects and ills of the world. Guns, knives, cars, and clubs do not kill; only people kill. Alcohol, inadequate education, drugs, and economic recession are accused of causing suffering, homelessness, divorce, unemployment, and countless other social problems. Our culture professes that no one is responsible for anything, with everyone merely a casualty of society's failures. Hence, no one has any control over their life-situation or individual actions, since we are all merely powerless victims of our environment. Such a belief is utter nonsense. People that abuse these inanimate objects are to blame. Inanimate objects do not inflict harm through their own volition. They do not cause suffering, except when carelessly misused or abused by humankind. Nothing happens on its own without direct action by people erroneously utilizing or abusing those 'offending items' within society.

Problems are not integral with society, or the objects it possesses, but with one's lack of self-control, discipline, and refusal to take responsibility for their own actions. Often times, such irresponsibility stems from an essential lack of understanding of our purpose and goal in life. Life is not obliged to protect us from our own failures and aberrant actions.

We can not all be victims or 'damaged goods,' and certainly are not merely products of society. Perhaps none of us had an ideal childhood or upbringing, and blaming our parents or environment for our present problems seems natural. Society's present 'recovery movement' has exploited this belief (or weakness) within an unenlightened populace. But embracing such a notion can be paralyzing, falsely believing that nothing can now be done, since damage has already occurred and we are encumbered with its effects as our 'burden in life.' One then simply accepts their state of arrested development, resulting in an absence of any correction or growth.

Regardless of our past, when adulthood is reached, let go of adolescence. Accept ensuing maturity, along with its accompanying wisdom, moving forward with life and the trials that confront us. If such engagement is not attempted, one will remain trapped within the past, in a self-imposed prison. We all have the ability and strength to cope with and overcome our hardships and difficulties. No life-path trial is ever intended, presented, or encountered that will be beyond our present endurance and capability. Physical life always provides us with the innate ability to endure and overcome such trials. Seek positives within those negative situations that are encountered, and learn their intended lesson, becoming more than what we are presently.

Despite past hardships, it is up to each individual to move on with life. No one else can live our life for us.

Realize that others have overcome similar past difficulties by coping, accommodating, and progressing through similar hardships, without expressing denial or blaming others. Adversity need not be destructive; it can also be a learning opportunity. Take control of life and its direction by rejecting victimization and accepting responsibility for what has happened, thereby taking appropriate action without punishing one's self over the past.

Discover what precipitated those negative occurrences, and implement corrective measures to forestall similar future events. Focus on the fact that such 'trials' can impart a better preparedness within our character composition, providing an expanded perception with which to view the future. Nurture spiritual strength, which can shield and assist us during those times of turmoil. Consider prior hardships as learning experiences when confronting similar events, using abilities gained from past lessons to overcome future trials. Each conquered obstacle provides further strength and experience for dealing with subsequent trials and lessons.

Self-responsibility promotes honesty and trust, producing the integrity to discern right from wrong, regardless of peer pressure. The opposite of 'accountability' for our actions is the secular concoction known as 'relativism,' a belief completely devoid of the absolutes of right or wrong. Relativism involves abstract freethinking, rationalizing that no one is ever responsible for their actions, with everyone merely a casualty or product of something beyond their control. People holding such beliefs tend to promote mostly liberal political views and socialistic tendencies, while often harboring agnostic thoughts or atheistic convictions.

Take full advantage of 'object lessons' throughout life, allowing those intended learning opportunities to ensue. Physical life permits us to become more than what we are presently. Our current life-path will never contain any event or obstacle that can not be overcome, as long as we continue to function at our highest level of current development and enlightenment.

Since each of us is developing at our own unique pace, our present abilities and character composition are the only assets that can be utilized to combat future obstacles encountered along our life-path. Therefore, focus should be on our own actions, not those of others. Comparing our abilities or life situation with those of another serves no purpose. Such comparisons are always dangerous, instilling false values, distorted perspectives, and conceit or envy. It further tends to allow the belief that one is 'above the law,' the laws of society and the Natural Law of Right and Wrong, or Good and Evil. Such a false perception then allows one to believe that rules apply only to others, not to them.

This dangerous practice of 'comparison' fosters attitudes prohibiting and deterring personal growth. It condones deviant actions by rationalizing that our deeds are not as bad as those of other people, therefore our actions are not actually wrong or evil. We further rationalize that our transgressions are occasionally permissible, since most of our actions are basically good and well intentioned. Committing deviant acts is always wrong, and will inevitably require some form of repayment, either now or in the future, based on the universal cause-and-effect laws of karma.

By comparing our present life with others, we discount what trials and hardships other people may have already overcome during a previous life, or what specific lessons they may be presently undertaking. We are all on a distinct path within our own development, in which we alone establish our timetable for correction and ultimate growth. We choose or agree to our own trials and lessons encountered during each successive incarnation, prior to returning for our next existence. Such self-acceptance is based on our individual need for certain correction, or added reinforcement of a specific behavioral trait. Current life-lessons are always predicated upon the presently obtained abilities of each individual, with no lesson beyond their current endurance or comprehension. It is each individual's responsibility to master their particular pre-planned trials.

Similar to 'comparison' with others, it is also crucial that one avoids 'judging' others. Since individuals are all developing at separate and differing rates, such a practice is dangerous and counterproductive. It creates false opinions and impressions of our own development, by contrasting our actions with those of another. That will always result in false judgment, similar to the proverbial apples-to-oranges comparison, since there will always be individuals existing at greater and lesser levels of development during our present life. Hence, an evaluation of our actions or 'worth' when judged against those of another can only result in distortions. It always produces false vanity or bitterness, providing neither positive purpose nor tangible growth.

We implement our own schedule of development through acceptance of our pre-planned lessons, and consequently may simply be proceeding faster or slower than others around us. Our focus must be on our own development, not meddling with the growth of others, or judging their actions. Any judgment directed toward another is a moot point, serving no purpose. While other people's actions may repulse us, we are equally unaware of that person's motivations or underlying intentions associated with their deeds, or their present level of character development.

The only true judgment occurs at the time of review over our most recently transpired life, between physical cycles of incarnation. At such a point, self-judgment is most valuable, since our true enlightenment level is fully restored, with all past memories, experiences, and insights. That allows an overview of all lifetimes that have comprised each entity, leading to an accurate personal assessment of one's progress and remaining deficiencies. We are only allowed to judge our own behavior, since each individual knows the true intent that was associated with all their committed deeds, as well as their personally obtained 'level of understanding' used to discern right from wrong. Honesty will always prevail, since we can not lie to ourselves.

At that time of judgment, our fully awakened perspective is restored, reuniting our soul's *Ka* and *Ba* and revealing the total scope and nature of all past accomplishments, as well as failures during our cumulative journey toward our ultimate goal of perfection at the Master Level. It also exposes an awareness of all remaining deficiencies, as well as those that have been corrected.

From such an awakened enlightenment level, the desire for a 'charmed' or 'easy life' would be viewed as non-productive, one without meaning or purpose. It would waste time and cause delays in the development of our innate character. With an understanding of life's grand purpose and awareness of our true perspective during this enlightened assessment process, such insight would certainly influence our selection of future life-path occurrences by picking event lessons with greatest personal value, based on our personal needs.

We must recognize that our present earthly perspective is quite narrow and protected from true reality. That clouds our scope and ability to envision the larger picture. Such a condition is due to the universal imperative to eliminate past influences that might affect our future choices and actions. That prevents each newly incarnated individual from falling into the same 'traps' they had previously established and nurtured, which would only lead to repeating similar past failures throughout their present life's lessons.

Every accomplishment achieved during subsequent physical life is merely an individual step, one taken within our immortal journey. Each reincarnated physical life is merely a single frame within the overall content of our 'eternal movie.' Life is never a one-shot existence; it is a continuing building block approach where we utilize our present lessons as 'managcable' stepping stones, in an effort to reach our desired destination of perfection at the Master

Level.

The development of one's core essence requires constant nurturing, in order to eventually achieve that ultimate goal. By learning from trials encountered during present life, each successive future life can become slightly easier, since we retain all previously achieved aspects associated with past deficiency corrections. Such a cumulative effect promotes future intuitive and ingrained responses to many of life's common and ever present adversities, thereby minimizing the impact of those obstacles whenever they are subsequently encountered.

As previously stated, each unique and distinct entity must master or overcome essentially the same lessons and trials as all other souls during their quest to obtain perfection at the Master Level. While specific events may be different for each individual, their content, purpose, and intent are essentially the same. Some trials may be learned the first time they are encountered, thereby establishing a permanent positive character trait within that individual. Or other trials and tests may be repeatedly confronted throughout many future lifetimes, with continued difficulty in mastering their specific lesson. We may constantly repeat unhappy lives, due to stubbornness or an incorrect perspective on life, refusing to identify or accept any responsibility for our personal correction.

Likewise, negative behavioral traits are learned and acquired during this same process. The accumulation and retention of ingrained negative traits always requires further lessons and trials in order to overcome their influence, before such correction can become permanent. To obtain the flawless 'Good' Master Level, we all must undergo this same step-by-step building process by overcoming common obstacles in order to achieve our permanent character trait perfection.

Humanity seems cursed to learn mostly from difficult trials, and seldom from easy ones. Instead of bemoaning a rough and difficult past or envisioning one's self as a martyr (at least within our own mind), be grateful, perhaps even thankful for such a challenging and difficult life. Appreciate the multitude of learning opportunities such a harsh life-path can offer, with its numerous hardships and trials from which correction and growth may more rapidly ensue. Such a recipient was deemed sufficiently enlightened to confront those tests, and was also adequately 'developed' to overcome and master their specific character deficiencies highlighted by those trials; perhaps finally allowing permanent correction of those specific retained flaws.

It can be difficult to perceive from our present perspective that we may have actually requested and agreed to such a difficult life-path during the planning of our present corporeal existence. While on the 'other side,' we are at a fully expanded enlightenment level, entirely aware of the larger picture. If indeed reincarnation is the universal reality of immortality, comprehend the insignificance of a mere single lifetime of hardships when compared to the magnitude of repeating multiple incarnated life cycles with minimal opportunities for learning and growth. One lifetime is merely a grain of sand in our hourglass of eternal existence, a mere tick of our ethereal clock, or merely a drop of water in that cosmic ocean.

To achieve significant correction and growth, a single lifetime involving enhanced lessons or hardships would seem a small price to pay. Such a life would offer many opportunities for accelerated progress, perhaps with enhanced focus on specific elusive character flaws, with the possibility for permanent correction of those 'chronic' deficiencies.

However, it is the responsibility of each individual to prepare for such hardships and trials, whenever they might occur during life. No life is ever risk-free or always fair; and no secular law can ever alter those facts. Plan, implement, and proceed with the life-path you previously accepted, ever mindful that negative occurrences can and will happen. Cope with such hardships by relying on your inner strength of character, one's personal 'reserve' intended to deal with such eventualities. Not all 'hardships' are unforeseen. Each of us will eventually grow old, so plan for its eventuality prior to becoming elderly. When 'ripened with age,' do not blame others that old age came unexpectedly. Do not rely on others to do what you should have done for yourself, or merely curse your fate and blame life's unfairness.

Always take responsibility for your own life. No one else is going to save you. Everything is left to each individual. The commitment to who we are, what we desire to become, and our actions taken to accomplish those goals are all products of our own choosing. That duty is solely ours. No one else is our caretaker, or a source to blame for our failures. We hear of people 'trusting in the Lord,' but such a belief goes only so far. On the premise that there is only one single, all-powerful, all-knowing, and all-loving God, without refuting or promoting such a concept, one must question the wisdom in relinquishing their personal salvation to some one else. Such an act rejects personal accountability, thereby abandoning individual control over the direction and outcome of their own fate.

The Creator does not interfere or intervene with the developing events encountered along our life-path, or influence our choice of actions taken in response to them. If one's God were actively involved, why would He allow wars to occur, killings to happen, and diseases to ravish entire nations? Why would He allow crooks, felons, and other law-breakers to enjoy the same societal advantages that good citizens enjoy? Why permit the rich to prosper even more, while the poor become more disadvantaged? God seemingly would not be so conflicted, displaying a split personality that is simultaneously both merciful yet vengeful, for no apparent purpose.

If one were to sit in a chair placed in the middle of a busy expressway, believing their God will intervene and protect them from the traffic because that individual has 'turned their life over to God,' they are sure to 'meet their Maker' sooner than expected. The Creator bestowed within each of us the ability to take care of and provide for our ultimate preservation. Instilled within all of us is the minimal wisdom and instinct to protect ourselves from harm, allowing us to learn, correct, contribute, and grow. The rest is up to us. Divine intervention was not intended, nor does it exist, regardless of how one chooses to perceive or explain life's unfolding events. No one is going to save us from ourselves. Regardless if one chooses to believe the opposite, the Creator does not intervene with anyone's life-path or free will choice. Such intervention would take away any personal responsibility for our own direction and choices in life. Perhaps those rare occurrences suggestive of possible 'divine intervention' may represent a form of assistance by entities above humans, but below the level of the Creator.

Do not look outside yourself for answers involving your own salvation, personal survival, or the corrective measures necessary to eliminate flaws and deficiencies. Expectation of outside assistance will always diminish the personal effort one expends toward overcoming any encountered obstacle. That is not to imply that we should never accept outside help, or offer assistance to others, but such efforts or interventions must be considered 'unexpected support' that is not anticipated when dealing with our specific life-path obstacles.

Responsibility starts with a proper perspective; realizing that others are not at fault and no one owes us anything. We must recognize that the things that can be altered within life are all fully within our own control. Life simply involves accepting the task at hand as it unfolds along our life-path, addressing those trials with our best effort to achieve learning and correction.

Responsibility involves getting back to basics, to a more sustainable manner and standard of living. Perhaps that involves a simpler material life style, concentrating more on our spiritual component and the real possessions of value such as positive character traits, which transcend time and the physical realm. Such an 'uncluttered life' with fewer tangible complications allows focus on eternal priorities, rather than on short-term material gratification. Avoid temptations to join the modern 'bumper sticker' mentality of obtaining the most earthly 'toys' as life's purpose. Such a pursuit only provides a diversion from life, in a misguided attempt to obtain happiness by running away from life's realities, without actually embracing anything of true value.

I am puzzled by society's propensity to hire others to perform most of their service work, including lawn care, car washing, repairs of all types, house and garment cleaning, and so forth. Then they join health clubs to expend the energy saved by hiring others for those services. Such action makes little sense, with no personal satisfaction derived from personally completing such tasks. Strive to create efficiency within your life, allowing the luxuries of life to manifest in your positive thoughts and actions toward others, not in material goods or the latest fads of society. Take care of the basics, and they will provide all that is needed.

The aforementioned areas of responsibility are predicated on each individual possessing unimpaired physical and mental functions, along with their ability to exercise free will choice. Self-responsibility always depends on one's capacity to understand right from wrong, while also being aware of the underlying intent associated with each action. Sometimes aberrant behavior may be due to physical or biological causes. Certain malfunctions within the brain's temporal lobes or its frontal region can alter both judgment and one's resultant responses.

Tumors causing brain damage or destruction of the hypothalamus, the regulatory control center of the brain, have been found to cause uncontrollable derangement. Such physical and mental impairments that affect one's behavior may be caused by congenital defects, later-life injury, or even from self-imposed causes including chemical or drug use (or abuse), or injuries resulting from one's own carelessness. Behavior associated with such self-inflicted action places its responsibility solely with the individual, perhaps as a lesson from which learning might occur.

In cases of biological derangement not associated with self-inflicted actions, the purpose and intent of resultant aberrant behavior is less obvious. Such occurrences do not suggest that merely bad luck or 'genetic-chance' were involved, since life's events always have purpose. Such events may be some sort of learning experience beyond our present comprehension. Or, perhaps that specific physical body may have provided certain prior learning experiences only offered by the life-path of that unique vessel, even though later life would involve physical impairment.

Such a physical life may also be a retribution for some prior heinous deed, one intended to help balance karma. Or it may even be a 'reward,' offered to someone seeking the perfection of Evil. It may even be an incarnation of a Master Level entity, returning to provide some unique lesson for another developing soul. Regardless of its intention or reason, all life provides some meaning and purpose from which learning and growth may result (in whatever direction that growth might aim). Such intentions are not always revealed, or perhaps even made apparent to the affected individual, although that entity did accept that specific life-path prior to rebirth.

Life's true meaning and purpose can not be found within philosophical pursuits. Rather, it is discovered by living life, with each successive life adding to one's cumulative composition. The qualities that provide for growth emerge from our positive interaction with others, through acts of assisting those in need and our contributions to the world. That is when life takes on true meaning, allowing positive gains from every life-path encounter. But do not plan every step in life or fight it along the way. Rather, live life as it develops, by being prepared for unexpected occurrences, and addressing those events as they occur. Each of us formulates our true character through small additions that occur from positive interactions in life, building step-by-step.

Look for strength from within, by following your intuition, conscience, or inner-voice that guide each of us. Such direction is within everyone. Never blame others for failures, or rely on others to 'save us.' There are no shortcuts, only dedication and hard work. Replace materialistic desires with a thirst for knowledge and meaning. Focus on living so that every physical existence matters, with some tangible contribution resulting from each life. Interact with life so that each of us can become a part of the greater universe, fully connected with all other souls in harmony. Any frustration resulting from 'daily events' manifests from our inability to perceive life as a learning opportunity from which correction and growth can ensue.

Confucius believed that men should seek virtue for its own sake, rather than some promise of reward within this life or the next. I believe that humankind can and will obtain a level from which they choose to do the 'right things,' not from fear of punishment or promise of reward, but simply because it is the morally intuitive way and correct manner in which to live. Long ago Aristotle wrote: "So the good has been well explained as that at which all things aim."[2]

Conceivably we will eventually choose to live a life reflecting Aristotle's belief, by being the best we can be within our presently obtained enlightenment level, without any denial or excuses. Such a life would not dwell on past mistakes or transgressions, since our best efforts were put forth at all times, always learning, correcting, and progressing toward perfection. Such a life could simply be based on the Golden Rule: *Do unto others, as you would have them do unto you.*

Chapter Eleven

Mysteries of Life

I would never presume that this writing has exposed universal truths for many of life's questions and mysterious ways. No attempt was made to address the scope of such a massive task, or to foolishly suggest any finite answers or solutions. The intended desire was to evaluate and offer alternative concepts pertaining to the very nature of physical existence, when viewed with an opened perspective, hopefully sparking further inquisitiveness on each reader's part to more deeply explore those areas of personal interest and intrigue that may have surfaced. As modern science strives to unravel and explain certain perplexing aspects of life, postulating plausible new explanations for such phenomenon, additional new mysteries tend to arise, which continue to elude understanding and full disclosure. However, if one is developing and progressing as intended, perhaps it is of no real importance to presently have all those answers.

Such searching and discovery may even be counterproductive, by overwhelming one with details. Many of us can not understand the inner workings of most modern conveniences, yet that does not preclude our use and enjoyment of those devices. I contend that all of life's realities and answers will naturally unfold when we are ready and capable of fully understanding them, as well as dealing with such revelations. Solutions will then appear as simple and basic answers, when perceived from such an enhanced or enlightened level of comprehension.

Since creative thought and logic first developed many millennia ago, greater intellects have tried to explain these mysteries of life. Perhaps an understanding of life's mysteries was never meant to be revealed to humankind while in mortal form. Conceivably, disclosure of such knowledge might disrupt the very balance within the universe, or perhaps one's personal development. Such revelations might create a paradox that could drastically alter the basic intent of physical life itself. Perhaps humanity, as an entire group of developing beings, simply has not yet evolved sufficiently to comprehend or cope with such complex disclosures.

In any case, further unknowns will be explored in the final chapter, only as food for thought, with no intent of offering speculative answers to such mental meandering. It is the nature of humankind to ponder life's mysteries, constantly seeking answers to those inexplicable occurrences. Perhaps that trait is the central catalyst that drives humanity's discoveries, inventions, solutions, resolve, and rationalization within the realm of the unknown. Through mere accident on my part, perchance a reader might be moved to explore solutions to one or more of the inexhaustible mysteries of life, thereby resulting in new revelations that would benefit humanity.

One of the most fundamental mysteries of life pertains to the existence of God. Human nature has an uncanny ability to find something, even when it might not exist. When humanity wants to believe in something strongly enough, new findings and results derived from empirical observations are then interpreted as coinciding or supporting that desired theory. Such conclusions may not be proof, but merely the power of suggestion. Any irrefutable proof always requires solid, verifiable, and reproducible results, with conclusions that can be documented from multiple independent observations. Humankind has never been able to prove the factual reality or even the self-evident truth of God's existence. God either chooses to remain shy around humankind, or such a concept, understanding, and tangible reality may simply not be possible while within human form.

If such an entity exists, does God direct everything, as would a puppet master? Or does that Supreme Power merely function only as an 'Originator,' with no further control over Its ensuing creations? If God once existed, does It still exist? For that matter, is it all that important to have total agreement as to how humanity categorizes, defines, or describes God, thereby establishing a common or universal image for such a Supreme Entity that is acceptable to everyone? Likewise, is it important to evaluate and compare the doctrine or canon associated with each of the world's various organized religious beliefs, ranking the merits of any single belief over that of another faith?

The argument over which God is the 'correct deity' immediately vanishes when one simply refers to such an entity as the 'Creator.' It becomes universally accepted that such a single Supreme Entity, the Creator, was the ultimate intelligence and planning force behind the Big Bang event that produced our physical universe, along with everything else within our domain.

Such argumentative differences are reminiscent of the universally known novel and movie, *The Wizard of Oz*. The wizard was certainly not what Dorothy had envisioned or even expected. He lacked the powers and potential Dorothy and her friends had first conferred upon him without having ever met him. Although he was nothing similar to their expectations, he still granted them what they sought. Religious concepts of God may follow a similar distorted expectation.

We may become too rigid in our beliefs and expectations, thus closing our minds to other possibilities and explanations. We overlook the main purpose of any given concept, focusing only on the methodology and nomenclature employed to promote its theory or belief, becoming lost in the semantics of such topics. It then becomes easy to demand uniformity and compliance from other competing beliefs, expecting universal agreement.

Is it most important that everyone puts their left shoe on before the right one, or is it more meaningful that shoes are worn to protect and support our feet? We lose sight that there are many ways in which to accomplish any task. While some may be more efficient than others, the real importance emerges with the ultimate accomplishment of those tasks. The same is true with our spiritual evolution and character development. Although some other approach to life might be different than our own, if they both eventually obtain correction and knowledge through their own process and direction, perhaps even after many laborious attempts, the desired end result or goal was still accomplished, ultimately fulfilling life's true purpose.

One's personal belief in their God or Higher Power is no different. Most religious concepts of God conjure up a human-form image, because we have been told that God created man in His own image and likeness, but which image and likeness? Is it one with the appearance of man as an adult, or as a baby, or perhaps as the first 'ancestor' within our family lineage, *Homo erectus?*

Without that necessary specificity, perhaps God's image is one of 'spirit form' only, just as the fundamental underlying form of humankind is its spiritual composition, our true essence as an eternal soul of 'pure energy' consciousness only. Such a lifeforce is capable of inhabiting both the physical as well as the spiritual realms.

Too often we jump to conclusions based on how we imagine things to be, and seldom contemplate true reality. Would God be any less a Supreme Power if depicted as the collective consciousness of the universe, rather than some bearded wise and mature man dressed in flowing white satin, seated on a golden throne while floating on a cloud? Perhaps such a conjured image is merely suggestive of a *Wizard of Oz* expectation.

The Creator still exists, regardless of how one imagines or perceives that Supreme Entity. Is the God of the Christian faith different from the Hindu God, or the one of the Islamic faith? Is there another deity of lesser or greater power that oversees alien cultures and civilizations on other planets in far away galaxies? Are there multiple Gods? Which concept is correct?

It is difficult to understand how religious believers can be so vehement, so radically opposed to others that do not mirror their own opinions. Is it truly importance for everyone to believe in the same divine concept? Or is the true importance of spiritual belief to impart comfort, purpose, and guidance within the lives of its followers, instilling a desire to strive for Good rather than Evil? If a spiritual belief in 'crushed pecan shells' produced a positive influence within someone's life, then such a belief would have served a beneficial role, similar in function to the basic purpose underlying any religious or philosophical thought.

Any religious belief should support the pursuit of truth, knowledge, and discovery, not its suppression. Followers of many religious beliefs tend to literally accept its ancient narratives, which have been handed down since their formative times, in an attempt to find some ambiguous 'proof' in those writings. Perhaps such accounts were originally intended to be 'teaching aids,' with their later distorted interpretations creating impediments to their initially intended lessons. Although any chosen conviction should suit each individual, there is still only one Creator. But humanity's history reveals a focus on the differences between competing religious beliefs, often resulting in warfare, rather than their common belief in the Creator.

Humankind must learn to embrace the many commonalties and similarities that universally exist between various religious factions, if peaceful cohabitation of our planet is ever to become a reality. Humanity's debates on the substance, nature, and form of God is a moot point. If mortal humans were actually meant to understand the true essence of the Creator, or perhaps the interworkings of the universe, such knowledge would seemingly have been exposed by now. An individual can still be spiritual and righteous without believing in an organized religious creed. Morality must originate from within each individual, not merely from an external belief in a particular religious dogma and its concept of a cosmic Godhead. Such influences can undoubtedly aid in the formation of ethical behavior, but such positive traits must be embraced and ingrained by each individual, going beyond the act of merely being exposed to such dogma.

Be comforted with a belief in a Higher Power, regardless if such a Force is called Yahweh, Allah, Jesus, Brahma, Atum, Ahura Mazda, or numerous other names. Or if such a Supreme Entity comprises the collective content of the universe, including a group of Masters. It is much more important to live a life that generates integrity and esteem from one's actions and contributions, rather than antagonism and frustration toward others possessing opposing beliefs. Always strive to live a life reflective of your best efforts and intentions, one seeking self-improvement that will lead to continual learning and correction, rather than seeking some promised afterlife reward for merely doing what is 'right.' Eternal rewards will surely be derived from any effort to correct retained character deficiencies. No longer having to repeat similar trials during future life-paths will be one immediate benefit, eliminating additional lives filled with anguish and disappointments.

Does any 'mere mortal' truly believe their character composition is sufficiently 'perfected,' without any corruption or loathing toward something or someone, to be worthy to inhabit the eternal realm of heaven? Is it even possible to obtain such physical perfection during one lifetime, a level of perfection that would not tarnish or diminish such a flawless heaven? While reflecting on such a humble concept, one will realize their many remaining faults still requiring personal correction.

With that realization in mind, were canonized saints

within the Christian faith, or other such exemplary individuals of other beliefs, simply rare exceptions of physical goodness overcoming evil within a single lifetime? Or were such extraordinary people merely nearing their 'final' evolutionary phase toward their perfected Master Level, reflecting growth achieved over many prior lifetimes of personal effort and correction?

We perceive death as the ultimate closure. If humanity truly possessed a firm conviction in an idyllic heaven, they would be dying left-and-right just to enter such a divine realm, and Dr. Jack Kevorkian, our nation's most pathetic pathologist, would be the most sought after celebrity. But most still harbor an abhorrent fear of death, which is merely the inevitable culmination of physical existence, with the true nature of afterlife, if any, remaining unknown. Death can be a release, perhaps even a welcomed one, from the pain and incapacity of illness. But it must never be the goal toward which we aim. Such a false pursuit would negate the purpose of mortal life, distorting its use as a mechanism of learning and correction during one's chosen life-path lessons.

Dying is not difficult. The act of living is difficult. Mortal life separates us from our eternal connection with the universe, from that collective consciousness we recognize as the Creator. Its symptoms are similar to the trauma experienced when a baby is separated from the comfort, security, and warmth of its mother's womb. Dying returns us to our origin, reconnecting us with the lifeforce of the universe. That act once more recombines both our physical and spiritual consciousness, which allows us to again become 'whole' when returned to our origin. To quote once again from T. S. Eliot: "We shall not cease from exploration and the end of all our exploring will be to arrive where we started and know the place for the first time."[1]

However, one should also understand that a certain degree of trepidation toward death is not only healthy and necessary, but also innate to the existence of physical beings.

Death instills a natural fear that helps keep one alert so as to avoid bodily harm and premature death. Such cautiousness provides a minimum of protection, allowing fulfillment of physical life, with its exposure to all life-path lessons as intended. As with all aspects of physical life, moderation is the necessary element. Any preoccupation with death can become a diversion, distracting us from learning the lessons offered by life's encounters. Although learning can occur while in the spiritual realm, it is within the material world where such lessons have their greatest impact.

The term 'spiritual' tends to invoke a religious connotation. Instead, think of the terms 'spiritual' and 'spirit' not in their traditional religious inference, but rather as a dimension of discarnate 'pure energy,' or a disembodied essence of consciousness. Such a 'non-religious' use of the term refers to the 'other side' where our core essence can also reside. Such a spiritual realm is the domain of true reality, where no intimidation by physical size or beauty exists. A place where insecurities spawned from real or imagined physical deficiencies can not influence any individual entity. A world where no other positive or negative aspect of one's physical body, the vessel temporarily housing one's essence, may be used as a tool or as a torment.

Rather, such a spiritual domain is where one's entire core character and collective essence is revealed. That realm is where we are in touch with our true self, with all our good and bad traits. It is where our complete consciousness is awakened, allowing recognition of our deficiencies as well as accomplishments. It is where one's next life-path lessons are planned, based on their remaining character flaws. However, we are not allowed to permanently remain within that ethereal domain until total perfection of our essence is ultimately achieved at the Master Level.

One does not grow towards death, but merely fulfills life, completing all their life-path lessons. No corporeal death is ever the end, it is merely a transition or plateau between periods of learning and growth. Physical death heralds the continuance and new beginning of further life-path experiences. It is within each mortal existence where we create our own heaven or hell. The choice toward either actuality is always left to each individual. One's obtained enlightenment level helps to determine the nature and severity of future trials and lessons within each life-path.

The arbitrary nature of life can often cause one to lose the sense of security that tends to ground each of us within our surrounding environment. Many times, one turns to religion to regain that sense of security. But any religion that is narrow and closed-minded, along with beliefs that are too confining and rigid, can impede one's direction and growth. That often breeds fear and resentment toward others holding different convictions, inciting thoughts of damnation, false perspectives or judgments, and even an apprehension of life within such myopic believers.

Any belief can become all consuming and detrimental. Be alert in recognizing any degradation within our character composition that might result from immersion within a new pursuit. Such narrow focus often promotes new vices that are even worse than prior ones that the latest pursuit intended to replace. Rigidity in any form prohibits growth by excluding one from experiencing life and its intended lessons, while also producing distrust, anxiety, and depression.

We should constantly be growing, or at least in the process of learning, to prevent any all-consuming pursuit from distorting our life-path events. Peer pressure also encourages similar myopic behavior, prompting individuals with low self-esteem to do things they know to be wrong and counterproductive. Such outside influences can be extremely damaging. Moderation can provide the necessary balance to maintain one's direction and conviction of purpose, when dealing with those more challenging life-path events.

Religion can also be used as a device to control people. Religion based on fear and control always represents a negative doctrine. Such notions impede humanity's quest for spiritual growth. Why would an all-powerful, all-knowing and loving Creator ever demand, or even desire homage or fear from Its followers? What possible reason or purpose would be served? No answer makes any sense. If the Creator had been merely seeking adulation or control over Its creation, It would have originally confined humanity within a corral, as a captive audience from which to derive such homage. Why 'convert' humanity if that was the intended goal, when the power for ultimate control already existed from the beginning?

The truly great men and women throughout history were all humble people that understood their limitations, as well as their potential. They accomplished their great deeds for the benefit of humanity, not for praise or recognition. Most likely their accomplishments were conducted without a desire for personal gain, but rather as contributions to humanity and the universe around them. Seemingly, their God would reflect a similar humble intent and character composition.

Too often humankind looks to God or organized religions for an easy fix to life's difficulties, rather than confronting those problems through their personal efforts of learning and correcting. Such 'quick-fix' concepts can also be utilized to take advantage of others. It seems that some questionable religious organizations are only interested in 'fleecing their flock' by prompting its followers into tithing, with a promise of a ten-fold return on such contributions. But their tenets require one to tithe first, before reaping any such beneficial windfall. A 'pay me now and trust me' sales pitch, the classic definition of a con-job. If some 'boiler room' investment firm or telephone solicitor made such claims, they would be arrested for fraud.

Any contribution of money, effort, or support directed toward any worthy cause should only be made because one believes in the intent and purpose of that cause, with true passion for its goals, and the good that might result.

Contributions should never be made with an expectation of any monetary gain or promised return involving some future reward for such action.

Humanity's prayers might also be categorized in a similar fashion. They may provide a false perspective that distorts reality. We tend to pray for what we want, or for something to happen affecting our life in some positive way. Those prayers may be motivated by an underlying consideration, perhaps one prompted by humanity's propensity for greed. Even one's best intentions may subconsciously be encouraged by this greed mentality. When we desire something, we have been taught to pray for it, thereby reducing such an act to merely another form of seeking the easy path in life.

No one else is going to save us, or provide for us. No one is going to intervene in our life trials on our behalf. Prayer will not alter what was intended, or change what must be learned. As individuals, we must take responsibility for our own life. People surviving natural disasters such as floods, earthquakes, tornadoes, or hurricanes often attribute their survival to prayer. But it is just as logical to assume that those who perished in those same disasters had also prayed for safety. If so, prayer accomplished little more than perhaps providing some spiritual comfort to those that ultimately perished. If one's life-path reached its conclusion, then time has simply expired for their current mortal period, and no amount of prayer will alter that reality.

We tend to seek the short cuts or easy paths throughout life. We ask for things that may be wrong for us, not assessing what in life is truly important. Rather, society constantly offers a quick-fix mentality of instant gratification, promoting overnight success and fame, crash diets, instant foods, and get-rich-quick schemes. But it is only through our own diligent efforts that we obtain what is truly worth possessing. Too often we do not comprehend what we ask and pray for. Prayer should only serve as a personal focal point, directing our attention and effort toward a given aspect of life, either physical or spiritual. That allows one to concentrate on their present task of required learning and correction. Perhaps such acts of 'prayer' may be more correctly termed 'meditation' or 'concentrated focus.'

Prayers that appear to be granted may result from one's own individual efforts, irrespective of any prayer involved. That statement is not an arrogant or self-centered humanistic perspective, one believing that mere mortals are somehow equal to a Higher Power. Quite the opposite, it is a very humble perspective on corporeal life, where we ask nothing for ourselves, but only for the wisdom to discern what is important in life. That allows correction of those aspects for which we are responsible, and the serenity to accept that which we can not change; based on our present developmental and enlightenment level.

For those believing in the power of prayer, they may merely be experiencing the effects from 'focused thought.' Concentration on a single element or goal perhaps focuses unseen mental influences from the power of one's mind toward a specific or desired outcome. Such focus has been shown to have a finite influence during experimental trials, resulting in achievement of a desired outcome, regardless if religious invocation or secular concentration was employed. Such directed focus of thought might have a real effect on an event, or it might subconsciously instill greater expenditure of one's own effort toward a specifically desired result.

For that same reason, I do not believe in religious-based miracles. They may not necessarily even be 'religious' in their origin, but merely a coincidence that suggests some connection to a personally held religious belief. Such events may simply be another of the many unexplained occurrences that are encountered throughout unfolding life. While such phenomena can not be explained within our current level of knowledge, perhaps their purpose and origin may be exposed to us sometime in the future, when our enlightenment is more compatible with such revealed truth.

Consider our present level of technology that is now taken for granted. It would appear to be some sort of miracle to past generations. Perhaps a more intelligent extraterrestrial species, in an attempt to aid our culture, cloaks their deeds and physical form in an effort to appear as the legends, myths, or religious figures we commonly envision and embrace. Such an advanced alien intelligence might even be mistaken for 'God.' While such beings may be far superior to present humans, they would not be the Creator. Perhaps Earth really is 'flat,' if we continually refuse to open our minds and perspective to all options within the realm of the unexplained.

Without an open mind, additional gains in knowledge will always encounter resistance, suppressing humanity's growth. Fortunately, humans possess an insatiable desire and energy for exploration and discovery. Perhaps by embracing an open-minded perspective, new discoveries might generate further understanding, either substantiating existing beliefs or revealing new concepts as a result of such enhanced wisdom. Those harboring doubts with their present beliefs are often more fearful to seek new knowledge and proof, fearing their beliefs may be proven wrong.

The potential exists within each of us to become more than what we are presently. Each of us possesses the ability to learn, correct, contribute, and grow beyond our present status. Too often we ask or pray for things that are beyond our current potential, seeking short cuts in life. No divine intervention will propel one beyond their currently attained level of development. Individual growth can only occur through correction of personal 'character deficiencies,' thereby equipping each individual with the necessary 'tools' to function at their next obtained level in life. That allows such an enlightened individual to then deal with life's more complex lessons.

Such progress becomes possible by focusing on the task at hand, while relying on one's determination and inner strength to achieve the necessary corrections desired. It also involves the ability to recognize those things that are simply beyond our present control. Likewise, self-help books and other popular self-improvement plans can not provide a road map, blueprint, or model for emulation; one describing some universal step-by-step procedure leading to such progress. Rather, it is the identification of one's faults and deficiencies, followed by application of dedicated effort to correct those flaws, when true progress will ultimately be achieved.

Lessons encountered along our life-path can be used as stepping stones toward that desired growth. By overcoming life's challenges and learning from those lessons, incremental progress is achieved with each individual step. Each of us, no matter how minimally talented, is capable of mastering some specific aspect of life. The magnitude of that journey will be minimized by taking only one step at a time within our larger mission toward perfection, with our remaining travel becoming more manageable with each successful step we accomplish over multiple lifetimes.

Through this stepping stone approach provided by the reincarnation process, everyone can obtain equally successful results through their own diligent efforts. As one masters a specific character trait, they gain knowledge and abilities, achieving new plateaus that can serve as resting points or rejuvenation places. Those plateaus also provide the time necessary for personal introspection, which allows one to refocus their efforts, while adding new vigor with which to interact with life. Such levels also reflect the period when corrective traits personally manifest, as they are infused within our innate character composition, providing greater pleasure and interaction during continuing life.

The resultant life is one in which actions are not forced, but flow freely and naturally from our more developed and defined character composition. Clearer meaning and purpose occurs from obtaining every higher successive plateau. The gains made from overcoming deficiencies then transcend from life to life as retained character traits, allowing our subsequent responses to become ingrained and 'automatic' toward similar future events. Such enlightenment allows each of us to experience a measure of contentment and solace within every future relationship. Physical life is not a race to establish the quickest time toward perfection. Rather, it involves measured and deliberate progress, along with absorption of life's many wonders and gifts. As higher enlightenment is gained from our life-path lessons, an enhanced appreciation of those material rewards also ensues. Perhaps one of our greatest gifts includes interactions and relationships with others. Such associations involve both love and acceptance, while also being devoid of any negative feelings of superiority or bias toward another.

If a relationship exists only because one party constantly does things to please the other, without similar reciprocity in return, then that recipient is merely experiencing self-gratification, not mutual love and respect for the other person. However, successful associations do not always involve equality or total agreement between committed individuals within a romantic relationship. Growth often ensues from honest disputes between couples. An open perspective always allows the views of another to be expressed; permitting consideration of new thoughts and attitudes that could ultimately result in a higher level of enlightenment.

True love can only exist between those who view their partner as an equal, while also recognizing the uniqueness of the other person. Such relationships often provide some of the best learning opportunities available. Take advantage of those special life-opportunities and their ensuing enlightenment, while perhaps creating or reinforcing a renewable association with an eternal soul mate.

Chapter Twelve

Science & The Unknown

As with any other spiritual or religious conviction, belief in reincarnation is just that, merely a belief. Any belief pertaining to the spiritual realm or some nebulous 'afterlife' can not be directly confirmed or disproved, but it is within humanity's nature to continually try. As of this writing, leading-edge science has attempted to prove the randomness, uncertainty, and paradox of the universe through application of quantum theory (aka quantum mechanics or quantum physics).

Quantum physics is the discipline or set of theories that explain the influence, composition, and interaction between subatomic particles, the smallest known fragments of physical matter such as leptons and quarks. Leptons form neutrinos and electrons, while Quarks act in a more complex fashion, first combining to form hadrons, creating two distinct classes, with one class becoming protons and neutrons. These tiny particles behave as waves, so the basic principals of wave-physics apply. This branch of science deals with the dynamic high-velocity behavior of these elementary particles, as measured in discrete units of energy known as *quanta*.

Quantum theory tends to indicate the possible existence of more than one simultaneous reality that might be associated with all events influenced by our free will choice. Such additional realities may exist on the spiritual plane, where one's essence or soul perhaps resides after death. Such a concept further links the condition of that spiritual realm to actions undertaken within our physical domain. Additionally, inevitable consequences from each and every tangible action apparently ripple through both the physical and spiritual realms, creating either harmony or chaos, depending on the nature or intent of each committed act.

Observations during experiments in particle physics have resulted in what is known as the Uncertainty Principle. This theory asserts that both the movement of subatomic systems and their location can not be simultaneously predicted. In other words, the location-in-time of such particles is uncertain, since any measurement to verify their position at a specific moment causes distortions, thereby altering their subsequent path and position. Hence, accuracy of their predicted movement, or the expected location of those particles can not be verified or observed with any repeatable exactness, due to this paradox.

Through application of this paradox, science has hypothesized that reality is not a local event. This theory has also been applied to events throughout the universe in order to show their randomness, contradiction, and uncertainty. Such an inference can be drawn from author and physicist Jeremy Bernstein's book, *Quantum Profiles*. The essence of its conclusions might best be described from a book review by Jim Holt, a New York columnist for the *Literary Review* of London. His review stated: "If there is an objective, cause-and-effect reality underlying the weird indeterminacy of the quantum domain...then it must be one in which events throughout the universe are instantaneously interconnected, as if by telepathy."[1]

As with most raw data, they can either support or undermine a hypothesis, depending on how those facts are presented. The conclusions in *Quantum Profiles* favored a totally non-connected, random, and disorderly universe, based solely on rejecting any unknown but instantaneous cause-and-effect force that might somehow exist within our vast cosmos. Such a conclusion relied upon Albert Einstein's (1879-1955) Special Theory of Relativity (1905), which postulates that nothing can travel faster than the speed of light. Hence, considering the vast distances encompassing the far boundaries of our universe, such an instantaneous interconnection would require some means of conveyance that would be vastly greater than light-speed.

But that same argument could also indicate that quantum theory does indeed advance the belief in a universe that is in total unity, one completely intertwined and interconnected instantaneously. This concept has now become a more widely accepted belief, which is thought to substantiate a certain underlying and instantaneously active force or phenomenon known as Quantum Entanglement. Such a concept is also quite similar to the doctrine of reincarnation.

Conclusions proposed in *Quantum Profiles* would negate the omniscient ability of a sole Supreme Divinity, thereby relegating planetary worlds situated within finite areas as having only a regional deity, not a single universal Godhead. Such thought has further spawned a new paradigm, the *Chaos Theory*, as an alternate view on life. That belief proposes that within the physical world, minute changes affecting the initial conditions of a developing complex situation can result in large consequences over extended time. Essentially, it is an opinion in which cause-and-effect is not relevant, since continuous flux-and-flow determines the only real outcomes from life's events.

Ironically it was Albert Einstein who refused to accept a universe devoid of a Supreme Being, stating, "God does not play dice [with the universe],"[2] believing in some instantaneously interconnected ability within the physical domain, although unable to scientifically prove that belief within his most recent life. However, such universal connectivity would require some unknown form of linkage or force that would vastly exceed the speed of light.

Although humankind's present technology can not produce propulsion that approaches or exceeds the speed of light, scientists have observed stellar matter comprised of subatomic particles within our own galaxy that were propelled at over ninety percent of light speed, due to influences from a neutron star or 'black hole.' Additionally, near-massless subatomic particles such as protons may be artificially accelerated within a long collider tube to more than 99% of light speed, as one intended purpose of the CERN Large Hadron Collider in Europe. Further, other experimentally generated light beams that vastly exceeded normal light speed of 186,282 miles per second have been reported, which were produced under specially prepared and environmentally enhanced laboratory conditions.[3]

Yet human imagination has envisioned and even predicted in books and movies such future achievement of velocities that could exceed that of light. Recall that it has been merely a tick of Earth's evolutionary clock since airplanes, rockets, submarines, computers, and trips to the moon were physical impossibilities, with experts proclaiming such fantasies to be scientific absurdities. Similar scientific authorities once promoted the belief that all stars revolved around a flat Earth. Therefore, nothing should ever be excluded, or thought to be an impossible achievement during some future time within humanity's continuing development.

Equally sound arguments can be postulated from the latest scientific discoveries and data, resulting in conflicting conclusions as to what could ultimately be achieved. Indeed, a persuasive hypothesis could claim that quantum theory essentially advances and proves that the universe actually exists in a state of complete 'oneness,' all connected and intertwined instantaneously. Such a condition would imply that every event anywhere within the cosmos would have an immediate consequence or affect throughout the entire universe, influencing all things within the physical realm. That is the very nature of the cohesive relationship that exists within our own solar system, as well as with other cosmic structures throughout the universe. Planetary orbits would constantly be altered, with random and chaotic positions, if such forces were not working as a universal cohesive and

206

connective influence on all such masses and their movements. Some think that gravity is the only natural force having such an expansive and immediate effect on matter. Perhaps some unknown yet-to-be-discovered dynamic force may also exist, providing both the potential and means for such instantaneous connectivity. The term non-random may best explain such an invisible interconnection. While the exact structure or composition of such an exotic force might not yet be recognized or fully understood, its association with material surroundings everywhere would likely have a definite pattern, purpose, and consequence.

Cosmic Connectivity

Perhaps one's enlightenment involves discarding material pursuits and connecting with some spiritual dynamic that can influence our actions. Physicists have utilized quantum theory to describe a mathematical model of the universe that might be a connection or bridge to ethereal knowledge. Such a connection might reveal a reality in which altruistic intent and actions would prevail. That reality could actually exist, regardless if presently discerned or not, with humanity somehow perceiving its intuitive truth. Modern neuroscience has apparently demonstrated how the human brain can instinctively 'know' something without our five senses verifying it with physical proof. Perhaps constant exposure to mundane societal distractions prompts us to discard, ignore, or distort such intuitive information or influence.

Some intrinsic connection apparently exists between our spiritual aspect (our soul), our brain (or mind), and physics. The Creator, the source of all intellect, is the most obvious connection between our known physical world and the spiritual realm. Science virtually concedes the Creator's existence through known mathematical laws and patterns that exist throughout the universe. Such predictable arrangement, order, and interaction was evidently conceived as a repeatable design within a Master Plan intended to govern the physical realm. Such protocols tend to indicate purposeful thought and a dynamic design behind the formation of our universe.

To understand the realm in which we live, we must first establish what is real and what may merely be an illusion. Such verification might be difficult while occupying material bodies, since everything within our physical world has mass. Gravity, the same cohesive force that binds our universe, also causes all mass to distort, skewing the 'reality' we perceive. What we see and seemingly understand is merely a distorted form of reality. Relying only on our physical senses for an accurate perception of life will simply result in faulty or incomplete beliefs.

Since the spiritual realm lacks mass, no physical force can cause similar distortions within that domain. Hence, true reality perhaps only exists within the spiritual realm. Every act affects and influences all else around, regardless if perceived or not. There are no private consequences from any of our actions. Each and every deed throughout the universe affects everything else.

A similar distortion affects time. Humankind tends to think of time as a linear commodity, wherein one event occurs after another, with subsequent outcomes building on prior occurrences. Since the physical world is an active realm that is ever changing, there can be no absolute time, only a time relative to events, and *vice versa*. Thus, all events must be described within some referenced time frame. However, time does not exist within the spiritual realm. It would have no relevance or purpose, nor could it ever constrain or limit any spiritual entity.

All actions within the physical realm must have a basis in time, although numerous infinite combinations of events may occur simultaneously within that same sphere of space-time. As an example, the light we view and recognize as a star tonight actually occurred at least 4.25 years ago, depending on that star's actual distance from our planet. That is based on the closest star to Earth, Alpha Centauri, a triple star system that is located some 4.25 light years away. In fact, most of what we view as having just occurred within our celestial kaleidoscope actually took place prior to our present-life's birth. Consequently, how can any mortal existence know true reality with any assurance, or be certain when a specific act or event actually occurred?

Thus, what we deem to be 'reality' from current events perceived within our material world must always be defined within some function of time. That is why a multitude of spectators may view the same event, with each perceiving a different reality, one that is relative to their own time frame of reference within their individual realization of that event. There is never a sole or absolute consequence that emanates from deeds committed within the physical world. Their effects will drift throughout all of eternity, and continue to influence all other physical mass that is eventually encountered.

Some theorists have even speculated that everything might be occurring all at the same time. That time might only be a 'localized event,' one that permits all things to happen concurrently, with every local event allowed to take place ever so slightly out-of-phase from all others. Such speculation would allow a specific physical space to be occupied on multiple different levels of consciousness or reality, all at the same time. Such a situation would allow all things to happen concurrently, as if superimposed one time period upon another, with each occurrence having a reality only within its distinct space-time interval for its specific inhabitants, or for some 'outside' spectator viewing that same designated time.

Time

Perhaps the commodity of 'time' only exists within the perspective of each individual. Maybe time does not actually 'flow' but might be static. Conceivably it may be each person that actually flows past the commodity of 'stationary' time. Considering such a perspective, time may merely act as a 'marker,' separating all events (past, present, and future) that occur (or have occurred, or will occur) at each specific location. Static time may have a 'layered' composition, with each layer containing all events that transpire at that given location, but are separated within their specific static time layer. As we live life, we merely 'index' through those specific layers of time relative to one's present perspective. Through use of free will choice, how one reacts or responds to each time-specific situation then determines the outcome of that occurrence or life-path event.

Such 'layered' static time might form a complex matrix of space, time, and events, wherein all things throughout time have already occurred. Through one's individual perspective, time then appears to unfold or flow, relative to each participant or observer, as they 'flow' toward their individually encountered events within such a temporal matrix of destined 'learning opportunities.'

Theoretically, a specific physical space could be occupied by an infinite number of different participants, experiencing individually distinct events concurrently, each within a different phase or layer of time that is out-of-sync with all other continuums. All participants would be creating their own time-based history, specific to their geographical location or 'space,' independently shaping their own indigenous reality, as other occurrences associated with that specific local are also transpiring at the same moment. Thus, a multitude of separate occurrences indigenous to each specific local, one for each different space-time period, would all develop concurrently within such a time-layering of past, present, and future history.

If 'time layering' or some similar phenomenon actually exists, then 'destined' events would be allowed to unfold for each unique space-time location. While on the 'other side,' when each individual chooses their necessary life path events for their next incarnation, a specific space-time period or 'life' could be selected. Such a life would allow anticipated life-lessons to occur, but permit each individual their free will choice in responding to those destined events. While indigenous structures confined to a specific locality would come and go over vast time spans, each time-layered event would have its own reality only within its specific portal of time. Hence, physical consequences associated with each point in time would have a physical reality only within its own time frame reference. Its specifically unique material structures and events would simply lack any substance or reality within all other time lines, although 'prior' history could still be evidenced from its fossil and artifact remains.

Under such a concept, physical consequences occurring during other time periods would not have an effect on that same physical location during other distinct time period realities. Thus, an archaeologist would not be crushed under the weight of a 'living' dinosaur from a past epoch, as it ultimately fell dead over the exact spot where that archaeologist would presently be unearthing the skeletal remains of that same beast. The ability to occupy the same physical locality or spot is achieved without interference, since each phase-altered 'dimension' or time sequence would have material reality only within its assigned time frame, even though simultaneous utilization of any given spot or location would be recorded for its unique time line.

Such 'time-layering' would be similar to cars on a highway that occupy the same physical spot of roadway, all without any interference (except in cases of accidental collisions), by being ever so slightly out-of-phase by a mere fraction of a second differential from the car in front and behind them. By considering the concept of such a layered time matrix, but experiencing only one of many realities contained within that out-of-phase continuum location, the

211

possibility of alternate realities within surrogate universes also becomes possible. Such realities may be overlaid on the same given spatial point of reference or location, or perhaps occur within another dimensional space-time existence.

Perhaps by unfolding those layers separating different dimensional realities, if indeed such realms actually exist, access might be gained from one space-time continuum to another. However, it is likely that merely one's spiritual component, not one's physical countenance or vessel, could actually traverse between those realms, or even be compatible within such exotic continuums of space-time, if they do indeed actually exist.

In a related fashion, perhaps one's spiritual consciousness could be embodied within a completely different vessel, another material body that is indigenous to an alternate space-time reality. But one's present body most likely could not survive such travel, let alone actually function in such an out-of-phase world. Perhaps separate components of one's consciousness might inhabit multiple existences on numerous planes of reality, all simultaneously. A vast array of possibilities that remain unknown to our present consciousness may become available within the astral domain. One might speculate that such revelations would only be exposed after humanity had gained sufficient enlightenment to cope with their associated complexities.

Hence, 'true reality' might not take place within our material world. We may merely be exposed to some 'perceived reality' that is relative only to a specific time frame. Occurrences would thus only have a true reality within the spiritual realm, as resultant effects derived from perceived life-path events encountered within specific time frames during physical existence are eventually experienced. Everything else would be merely sensory impressions or imaginings that are extraneously perceived by each individual.

Such events could be equated with viewing a celestial

star, where its influence or occurrence is perceived to occur only within the present, as it is processed by our physical senses. But the viewing of such an event actually transcends time and physical reality, with light emission from each star leaving its permanent effect on the cosmos. As such light wave photons become indelibly ingrained upon the layers of time, their consequences within the physical world also become eternal, providing their ability to be viewed by an infinite number of distinct beings during various and widely separated periods of time, even while on other inhabited planets.

Do consequences of viewing light waves from a twinkling star affect the universe on the night they are seen, or have their true impact actually taken place many years before when first emitted? The initial impact on the universe from those photons was recorded years ago when it first happened. But that same emission is just now becoming a visual reality within our location of the universe, thus influencing our present world. Yet it may continue to influence many other more distant planets sometime in the future, perhaps as romantic inspiration for a couple gazing into their night sky. Such waves of influence from a single action continue to ripple and drift throughout the universe for all of eternity, each with their own infinite number of effects and consequences over the eons of time.

Past lives may have been affected by similar previous acts, with their additional affects yet awaiting future lives. A comparable concept is being utilized by modern science in an attempt to view the origin of our universe, the Big Bang event, by peering into the outer reaches of the cosmos. The intent is to detect the start of that primordial occurrence by observing its early emissions, which are now within the scope of our scientific sensory ability.

Such cosmic observations of the Big Bang creation demonstrate that all actions since the dawn of time leave their continuing imprint as ripples of influence that affect future history everywhere within our universe. To better explain the factual reality of such indelible waves of influence, we need to evaluate the basic fundamentals of gravity as described by Sir Isaac Newton (1643-1727). Newton's 1684 Law of Gravitation states that the gravitational attraction between two bodies is directly proportional to the product of their masses, and inversely proportional to the square of the distance between them.

Through empirical observations, modern science has highlighted the incompleteness of this Newtonian theory. Modern application of quantum mechanics has amended and complimented Newton's gravitational theory, allowing a more complete prediction of its effects on our material world. A review of Albert Einstein's 1916 General Relativity Theory proves that gravity is not only a force of nature, but is also a geometrical distortion; one that is exerted in all directions upon the fabric of space-time. Hence, there are at least two known and separate components that are contributing influences for the force of gravity.

Prior Newtonian Law described the concept of gravity more in terms of an object being held in place, or pulled as if on a tether-line. More accurately, any mass causes the space-time fabric of our universe to distort or curve, forming a type of 'racetrack' indentation. Thus, all matter moving through the universe also follows a similar 'curved track' caused by the gravitational force of its own mass, as well as gravitational effects from all other masses that exist at the same time elsewhere within the physical universe. Such space-time distortion is what causes light to curve, and affects trajectories of all moving matter, although those effects are mathematically predictable with only minor errors. Hence, relationships between masses demonstrate both a 'distorting influence' as well as a force of 'attraction.'

Ostensibly, such forces also bind all events within the universe into a sphere of connection, with 'cause' having a resultant instantaneous and simultaneous 'effect.' Science further believes that a third component of some totally unknown nature might also exist in addition to the known components of gravity's attraction and distortion, which affect and influence all matter and their trajectories.

Cosmic Origins

The origin of our cosmos is a subject that has spawned much controversy and division between religious theologians and scientists for centuries. Yet those two sides may have more in common than ever imagined. The religious belief in a Divine Genesis and science's Big Bang theory have essentially been proven to be mutually compatible, at least in their respective outcomes, if not in their manner of deployment bringing about the agreed upon result. Humankind's thirst for answers, coupled with research and scientific advancements, has revealed data supporting agreement between these two seemingly opposing beliefs. Modern scientific evidence derived from studies of cosmic helium substantiates the theory of a cataclysmic explosion that resulted in the formation of our known universe, sometime between thirteen and fifteen billion years ago. Latest cosmological research has further refined this event as having occurring about 13.8 billion years ago.

Creationists and scientists alike may now share a common belief origin that assumes a finite beginning, and hence a genesis of everything that followed, all emerging from a central blinding flash of light. Quantum mechanics further suggests that such a universe was actively created, based on a predetermined mathematical formula. To comprehend the similarities within these two perspectives, a review of the latest technological findings will be helpful.

The largest and most ancient cosmic structures known are the thin clouds or 'ripples' located at the distant outer reaches of our universe. Such formations represent the earliest stages of matter clumping together, which were brought about shortly after the initial creation of the universe. Research work headed by Dr. George Smoot, an astrophysicist at Lawrence Berkeley Laboratory, has measured cosmic-radiation signals by means of NASA's Cosmic Background Explorer (COBE) satellite.[4]

Observations were made of numerous encountered energy remnants believed to be from the Big Bang's afterglow, which indicated that a colossal primordial explosion occurred more than thirteen billion years ago that led to the creation of the universe. Based on data gathered from hundreds of millions of measurements left by that afterglow, it was determined that an even distribution of temperatures existed throughout the cosmos. Since thermal radiation readings were essentially all the same when measured in every direction, it was concluded that all encountered energy remnants within the cosmos must have occurred from a single source.[5] To better understand this finite conclusion and the accompanying phenomenon that helps to explain our physical universe, a basic astrophysics review of the fusion process utilized by stars to produce their massive energy might be useful.

Stars 'shine' or emit light and heat (radiant) energy by nuclear fusion, a process that fuses the lighter element of hydrogen into the slightly heavier helium element. This nuclear synthesis converts millions of tons of hydrogen into helium every second, losing mass during the process. The 'explosions' associated with this process produce shock waves that propel pockets of gas through space at fantastic speeds estimated at three million miles per hour. Those gas pockets smash into other interstellar gases, causing their combined mixture to compress and superheat, thereby producing new ingredients to form additional elements. However, only the phenomenal pressure and heat of a supernova explosion, or something of similar energy production and release, can create the much heavier elements such as the various different metals.

But initially, 'dust' from collisions of elementary particles of quarks and leptons clumped together to create the first hydrogen molecules and ultimately the first star and its fusion process. Within the very early universe, as more dense elements were produced and carried outward by ensuing shock waves from expelled stellar gas, those heavier elements eventually combined with oxygen, carbon, and other necessary life-producing molecules through subsequent impacts with gas pockets in different regions of space. From continual collisions within those nucleating sites, debris enriched with the newer heavier elements was also expelled, ultimately forming additional new stars, planets, and moons, with at least one subsequent planet (Earth) eventually producing elementary life. There, under ideal conditions, through the process of cellular division, mutation, and evolution, higher forms of life including plants and animals eventually emerged. This rudimentary primer on basic astrophysics prepares us to better understand the concept of the Big Bang event, as described in the following explanation.

At the primordial beginning, some theorize that all physical matter in the universe apparently existed as a single point of compressed mass that was smaller than the head of a pin. Roughly 13.7 billion years ago, the center of that infinitely dense mass became superheated (how and why still remains unknown), rendering that 'supermass' unstable. The resulting cataclysmic explosion sent energy forces and fundamental particles uniformly outward in all directions.

A somewhat 'revised' account states that the central origin where the universe commenced had consisted of a lone point of pure energy, devoid of any matter and entirely without material composition. For some unknown reason, approximately 13.8 billion years ago, that concentrated quantity of pure energy underwent a superheated state, causing its instantaneous and massive 'release,' rather than a conventional 'explosion.' The ensuing cataclysmic liberation of such an immense concentration of energy created temperatures never experienced before or since, which forged the elemental particles that are thought to underlie all physical matter. Those subatomic particles were propelled outward, uniformly in all directions. Subsequent collisions of those basic building block particles later joined to form simple atomic structures, which eventually combined further on an ever-continuing and more complex basis, causing our cosmos to form.

Either explanation apparently involved subsequent chaotic collisions of those newly 'forged' fundamental particles, combining them into variously different forms during those impacts, allowing the continuous formation of ever-newer particles that ultimately created basic elements and cosmic structures. That process continues through the ongoing redistribution and refinement of those original components as a lingering result of that long ago initial energy release and inflation process, thereby further expanding our known universe, even during present times.

Conditions *before* and *at* the instant of ignition that produced the Big Bang event were completely different from what ensued later. The environment *before* that event remains totally unknown. Perhaps that point of origin (where the Big Bang occurred) emerged from the spiritual realm. While based within the physical domain, it may be impossible to determine the actual composition or characteristic of what existed before our material reality, simply because the laws, structure, and configuration of that different realm is likely incompatible with ours.

The unique conditions *at* that moment of ignition for the Big Bang event represented a one-time inferno environment that is thought to have produced all the fundamental particles of quarks and leptons, which later formed all the subatomic elements that now comprise all atomic structure. Instantaneously *after* ignition, that unique inferno condition expired, and has subsequently never again been duplicated.

Concurrent with that creative genesis, our physical universe also began its existence, which was the moment when our perceived laws of physics first started.

Deployment of this Big Bang process as the mechanism that created our universe is no longer in dispute, only the origin of power underlying such a process is now in question. Current debate associated with the Big Bang theory now focuses on the 'open' or 'closed' aspect of the universe's formation. Those disputes describe a 'closed universe' as growth or expansion to some distinct predetermined 'outer limit' only, as ever-increasing gravitational forces from its own mass finally 'contains' that long ago explosion. Such a scenario would ultimately produce a stationary or non-expanding cosmos, one that might even collapse back upon itself. Conversely, an 'open' universe is believed capable of continued inflation for all of eternity, never producing an ending, while ever expanding into infinity. The key element within such a debate rests with the determination of the so-called Critical Density theory.[6]

If the universe has just enough matter to produce a 'critical density,' then it will continue to expand only to a fixed point, albeit at a reduced rate of growth, due to the effects of gravity. Such a condition would eventually reach a near steady-state condition, one without perceived expansion. However, if the universe's density is below such a critical level, the universe would not be constrained, and would continue to grow larger for all of eternity, without concern of gravitational effects from its subsequent ever-growing amount of matter. Conversely, if the density present in the universe became greater than that critical level, it would eventually grow to such a size that it would reverse its expansion due to the growing effects of the additional gravity produced by its increased density, and likely collapse upon itself. In any case, the universe is presently far from approaching any 'critical point' for such final determination.[7]

The Big Bang refers to an instantaneously brief

microsecond of time when the universe was extremely hot and dense, followed by a continued period of expansion and cooling. Its origin apparently occurred within a single finite homogeneous point of space. Certain Sanskrit texts seem to suggest that the Creator may have spent an eternity as a single-point Source, or perhaps even numerous 'eternities' if such a quantity of time might actually exist. Some further speculate that the evolution away from such a single point of existence may have occurred as a result of the Creator's overwhelming loneliness caused by such long isolation. Hence, some believe that the Creator 'recreated' Its own essence through the energy release of the Big Bang event.

Modern science theorizes that the realm that existed before the Big Bang was perhaps a subatomic domain that housed a perpetual and unlimited Energy or Force. Before anything existed, perhaps there was only darkness within that nebulous ethereal realm, a domain that does not possess the commodity of time. Eventually the physical universe was created from the release of that underlying ultimate Force, which apparently originated from the thoughts and will of the Creator. Such a process would have essentially created matter solely from pure thought, through some incomprehensible energy conversion process that was part of a Divine Master Plan, which intended elementary particles to underlie all material composition in its eventual formation of an infinite number of subsequent physical commodities. Certain archaic evidence exists to support the creation of material reality through such a Divine Thought process.[8]

Those two domains, the original ethereal realm and the subsequently created physical one, are apparently somehow instantaneously interconnected everywhere within the universe. Conceivably, the Creator may have split-off small portions of Its own energy or 'consciousness' into an infinite number of 'spiritual elements' (perhaps souls), similar to the fundamental particles of quarks and leptons, in order to directly experience all that would unfold within the physical domain. Such 'ethereal elements' might temporarily infuse with each created material object, thereby directly and intimately knowing what those commodities 'experience.'

In the case of sentient beings, each individual 'soul' might then possess self-awareness, along with a unique personality, creative abilities, independent thought, and free will choice. Utilizing these infinitely numerous 'commodities,' the Creator would have the potential to experience all possible interactions, both Good and Evil, by being an integral part of each separate entity. That allows the Creator a 'dual presence,' connecting both the spiritual and physical worlds. That dual existence might allow the Creator to maintain constant and instantaneous contact with everything within both realms, ultimately experiencing first-hand all that transpires.

That perpetual contact and connection would confer absolute omniscience to the Creator, since everything any individual would ever learn, the Creator would also know. Physical life experiences would also confer similar knowledge back to the Creator, imparting that Universal Consciousness with an awareness of everything, both spiritual and physical. Such a plan would provide the Creator a unique ability to constantly expand Its consciousness, from an infinite number of available choices that emerge from experiencing all conceivable events and their resultant outcomes. Such a concept also allows each fragment of individual consciousness the ability to adapt to many different forms of physical life within a number of 'alien' environments. Such speculative 'mental meandering' is presented only as a catalyst to provoke further thought.

However, such conjecture and focus should not be directed solely upon the creation process only, but also on the thought and planning that proceeded the initiation of the Big Bang event. As a prerequisite of that event, the formulation of all physical laws, chemical reactions, biological interactions, and mathematical formulas were apparently conceived prior to initiating that grand genesis. Such a feat exceeds all physical comprehension, while invoking total awe with the intellectual grandeur that was ultimately involved with such a monumental undertaking.

Such intellect could only reside with the Supreme Creator. Since the Creator's preplanning must have occurred before the Big Bang event, the Creator can not be a physical entity, since no physical realm yet existed. Any later 'conversion' to physical form would only limit such a Supreme Entity, with subjugation to physical laws and forces. As such, the Creator can not be relegated to any known classification more specific than an 'It,' One without gender, form, or any other physical limitations. Hence, humanity's personification of the different physical gods referenced throughout the various mythologies of many ancient cultures, as well as physical gods described in many diverse religious beliefs, simply could not be that originating Supreme Force behind the Big Bang event, the true Creator.

All things in the physical world are comprised of smaller basic components, from subatomic size to macromolecular structures. Earlier in this chapter, it was revealed how fundamental particles produced by the Big Bang event eventually formed into base elements and still later combined to form ever-more complex compounds and structures. As physical commodities were ultimately transformed, eroded, or dissipated, their base essence would constantly be recycled into ever-newer creations. The same is apparently true for the subsequent sentient life that eventually emerged within the physical world. That physical life obtained cognition, thereby producing thinking and creative 'extensions' of the Creator. With evolution of human life, one endowed with the same or similar 'soul' or essence of the Creator, such life apparently also undergoes similar 'recycling' upon physical death. Reincarnation appears to be the process associated with that continued reclamation of all cognitive entities.

The physical realm was intended to manifest, develop,

and transpire without intervention from the Creator. The Creator's only involvement was in formulating the immutable laws governing the continuing and predictable events that would occur within the physical realm. The ultimate purpose of later 'thinking creatures' is to interact with unfolding events throughout life, utilizing one's free will choice while learning, correcting, and contributing to the physical world; with the intent of perfecting each individual 'component entity' for their eventual return and final reunification with the Creator.

It was always accepted that such a process would be a lengthy one, fraught with individual gains as well as personal failures. Such a physical perfection process would require numerous existences for correction of retained faults and deficiencies, as well as any new ones accumulated during those continuing lifetimes. Thus, 'immortality' was bestowed upon those thinking 'life elements.' That allowed all the time necessary for the learning, correction, and growth; which would be required to ultimately obtain individual perfection. But that obtainment can only be achieved through numerous existences. Such 'immortality' is provided through the process that humanity recognizes as reincarnation.

Perhaps the Creator revealed Its grand purpose for physical life to some primordial sapient species on an earlier planet within our 'younger' emerging universe. The Creator may have then commanded that initial species to reveal the intent of mortal life to all subsequent developing 'infant' lifeforms. Such an assignment may have involved sharing specific life-lessons in the hope that certain earlier mistakes would never again be repeated. There can only be one 'first time' when the 'wheel' is invented. Needless repetition of 'basic' mistakes simply makes no sense.

Later emerging species merely addressing the same problems that were encountered during primordial times would seemingly not be a productive use of intelligent resources, nor would it supply any meaningful contribution to the universe as a whole. Hence, it is possible that prior divine

223

intervention, utilizing higher enlightened beings from another dimension or world, may have actually imparted the Creator's intended purpose of life to some ancient earthly inhabitants.

Speculative Forms of Existence

The Big Bang genesis indicates that the universe is comprised of energy and matter, with matter being a condensed form of energy. The essence of our being or 'soul' may simply be pure energy, since it is believed to be ethereal. Thus, it has the ability to transcend corporeal life, having compatibility within both the physical and spiritual realms. Pure energy is not relegated to any specific shape or configuration, and thus may transform or incorporate into any form or type of matter desired.

Perhaps pure energy may also be capable of obtaining a quasi-physical existence, something between physical and ethereal, which might produce a partially visible illusion within the material world. Such a condition may account for the reported appearances of 'spirit apparitions' or ghostly images that some people claim to have observed. Speculating further on such a semi-corporeal state, perhaps thought projections from an enlightened essence may create the ability to be in more than one location or dimension at the same time, perhaps even 'taking over' or sharing another physical vessel. Such a condition is often referred to as a "walk-in" by some followers of reincarnation.[9] Perhaps humanity's future evolution may ultimately involve only our spiritual component, allowing amazing 'extra-physical' abilities presently beyond known understanding.

In the spiritual realm, pure energy or 'self-energy' need not be in any particular shape or form, and may be able to attain any conceived arrangement or pattern desired. Perhaps energy manipulation through molecular control might some day allow humans to obtain a quasi-physical or semi-corporeal state within the material world, ultimately allowing uniquely new abilities.

Physical World

While speculating over fantastic concepts and abilities that might be possible while within the spiritual realm, our vast physical domain also offers many wonders of its own to explore. It has been determined that much of the matter in space is not readily visible. Observations made by the ROSAT X-ray satellite indirectly indicate the existence of matter that can not be optically detected; a type that is essentially invisible to us, yet is thought to exist due to its discernible gravitational effects on surrounding cosmic bodies.[10] Such strange 'dark matter' may actually comprise the bulk of all mass within our physical universe. Existence of such matter has been postulated from observations of massive gas clouds that appear to be 'contained' by influences from an invisible gravitational field. Some scientists believe that the majority of this dark matter is made up of white dwarf stars. Such stars have burned out, drastically cooled, and will ultimately fully collapse internally, ever increasing their gravitational attraction.

Initially, possible evidence of this dark matter had only been assumed using 'gravitational lensing,' a process where a distant light source is bent as it passes through or near very massive structures while traveling towards its eventual 'observer.' Since dark matter is invisible and nonreflective, it can not be seen directly. Still, many scientists believed it existed, since galaxy clusters would separate from one another instead of traveling together. Now, finite confirmation of this exotic commodity has been directly observed. While using the Hubble Space Telescope in late 2004, a massive ring of dark matter about 2.6 million light years across was accidentally discovered while studying the galactic cluster within the constellation Pisces.[11]

It is noteworthy that the bulk of the matter comprising

most galaxies tends to concentrate or clump in a manner that forms an irregular ring or band near its outer peripheral boundary. Such an arrangement produces vast central voids within those cosmic arrangements, which can extend one hundred million miles or more, with similar voids also evident in 'empty space.' Some of these expanses are thought to contain this dark matter.[12] Such dense packing of matter may be due to, or perhaps caused by, such 'voids' harboring one or more black holes. A black hole is thought to be a densely packed concentration of mass having limitless gravity so nothing, not even light, can travel fast enough to escape its immense gravitational force and influence.[13] Yet the bulk of 'nothingness' once envisioned to be located within those vast central voids of galaxies and empty expanses of deep space may be comprised of this incredibly dense 'dark' matter.

Perhaps such voids might also contain thresholds into other worlds, leading to parallel or alternate universes that may be totally separate realms containing their own distinct reality, one different from ours. Or perhaps such voids may contain time-portals, or tunnels through space-time in the form of 'wormholes,' somehow allowing transport through our known space-time continuum, with arrival into other dimensions of reality, or even different time-periods (verging on time travel). Such speculation could also involve the theoretical concept of 'folding space,' which might permit displacement of great distances within the vast reaches of our cosmos, by temporarily 'rearranging' those locations into closer proximity, similar to a 'shortcut' route.

The evolution of our universe may be a gradual and progressive process toward some ideal state. Karmic balance might actually determine that rate of progress, based on cause-and-effect consequences resulting from daily physical life. The totality of our life-path experiences over all physical existences apparently leave 'foot prints' on each stepping stone used to traverse that journey. Each unique action imprints a permanent legacy as a record of all deeds.

Consequences from those deeds become permanently ingrained on the ripples of space-time, drifting throughout the universe for all eternity, with their potential to further affect future history perpetually existing.

Humankind has been a late occupant of our planet. The universe is estimated to be about 13.8 billion years old, formed as a result of the Big Bang event. But Earth is much younger at only approximately 4.7 billion years old. Science is in dispute as to the first appearance of what remotely could be called humanity's earliest ancestor, with that oldest suspected hominid dating between four and six million years ago as the genus *Australopithecus*.

That occurrence represents a sizable gap between the creation of our universe, the much later formation of planet Earth, and humanity's earliest appearance. Why did the Creator supposedly wait so long to produce intelligent life? Was humankind merely an afterthought? Was the first earthly 'humanlike' appearance also the initial existence of an immortal soul? Or might other lifeforms have once existed and housed such a spiritual 'soul-essence' long before humanity's more recent evolutionary introduction on Earth?

Over two hundred million years ago, dinosaurs ruled our planet. Therefore, if one's soul existed on Earth that long ago, it would seem logical that such an essence would have resided in some reptilian lifeform, the highest form of life on Earth at that time. If our soul existed five billion years ago, before Earth's creation, was it then housed within an alien lifeform on some earlier planet in a distant solar system? Perhaps if our essence was once housed by such non-human lifeforms, a future reincarnated existence might involve some new yet-to-be-created species.

Regardless, does it even matter if one's essence was once housed within a reptilian vessel, an ape, a caveman, or even an extraterrestrial lifeform; as long as learning, correction, and growth ultimately took place? As long as one's soul or essence is able to interact with life's lessons, then the

227

circumstances and settings for those occurrences seem to be of little importance within our ultimate ability to learn, correct faults, and contribute to society.

The most fundamental metaphysical mystery seems to be why there is a physical domain, instead of merely a discarnate one within a spiritual realm. Why is there 'something' instead of 'nothing'? Does one's spirit or soul exist concurrently in the spiritual realm while it also inhabits a corporeal body? Mathematics proves that two distinct planes may contain the same point, if that point is contained on the line of intersection of those two planes. Perhaps one's consciousness has a dual existence within both the spiritual and physical worlds simultaneously, as long as a constant point of intersection exists between both of those realms.

Perhaps mortal death breaks a personal intersection between those two dimensions, temporarily relegating one's essence solely within the spiritual plane. Perhaps our consciousness only exists in the spiritual dimension, and merely perceives the material world through the utilization of the physical senses employed by our host vessel, through some sort of remote sensory connection. Or perhaps there is no presently definable correlation that exists between our physical world and the spiritual realm, with those two domains being as foreign as Good and Evil.

The concept of reincarnation further opens a myriad of questions and speculative thoughts. Were all souls 'created' or 'born' at the same time? Or are there 'older' and relative 'newer' souls that came into existence at various different times over the ages? How might one account for Earth's varying population numbers, both greater and smaller, which have existed over various different time frames? Did certain souls perhaps stay longer on the 'other-side,' or might they have inhabited lifeform vessels on other worlds within distant galaxies during Earth's lower population periods? Through empirical observations, the noted astronomer Edwin Hubble concluded that our universe is constantly expanding in all directions, leading one to speculate that perhaps such new 'soul' entities may still continue to be created even now. Might 'perfected souls' spawn or create such new 'entities,' as a sort of spiritual propagation? And why is the universe expanding, and will it continue to expand throughout all of eternity? Also, what does such cosmic growth displace? Since there are theoretical boundaries to the universe, what lies beyond its edges? Does 'nothingness' occupy the space beyond known boundaries, or must 'nothingness' first be created to allow expansion into its region? One may speculate that the propagation of Good is the driving force in the expansion of our universe. Perhaps such growth displaces the realm of Evil, that area of 'nothingness' beyond our universe's known boundaries.

Or perhaps the unknown 'region' being displaced by cosmic expansion is that of the spiritual realm, a dimensionless 'void' that apparently can only contain pure energy. Such a domain would not have a definable territory, since it would lack any physical point of reference, one without a framework of spatial attributes. It also would not possess a temporal dimension or 'time line' of reference. There would not be any 'temperature' or other physical sensations, since matter would not exist within that domain. This realm could not be detected, since it would lack an energy signature in the form of electromagnetic radiation. Nor would it possess any mass that could be quantified. It apparently would be infinite, since it would lack any external or definable boundary for its containment. Such a spiritual domain would not be affected by the space-time continuum of the physical universe, since it would merely be moved 'out of the way' during the ongoing expansion of our physical cosmos.

Perhaps a harmonious relationship exists between these two realms, where they are somehow balanced, or exist in mutual equilibrium. Perhaps an eventual merging of these two dissimilar dimensions will someday occur, creating an entirely new state of personal consciousness or existence. But change by its very nature involves a function of time as it correlates with some form of energy exchange, or its conversion into matter, as well as any physical movement or displacement of distance. Hence, any combination of such diametrical realms must create an entirely new domain reality, one unlike either of its prior existing elements.

Any conjecture on such matters can only be highly speculative, and probably also the source of much laughter and ridicule. Such questions, as well as their elusive answers, become a moot point, striving merely to inspire thought and an open perspective, stimulating a desire for further examination, contemplation, and discovery. Attention must be focused on our present endeavor and personal responsibility to learn, correct, contribute to society, and gain enlightenment; the fundamental underlying purpose of all physical life. Hence, speculating on matters that are outside our control may simply become a meaningless distraction from our presently more important underlying task.

From my personal search to expose life's meaning and purpose, I arrived at the belief in reincarnation simply because it made the most sense, with the simplicity and clarity that I believe Galileo could have embraced. It is a belief rooted within the basic process of continual learning and correction, allowing growth and enlightenment at whatever pace an individual exerts through their own efforts. Reincarnation provides an ultimate fairness through the inherent balance of karma. The belief in reincarnation can also manifest as a way of life, imparting an understanding and acceptance of why things happen, and why others do not. Reincarnation permits acceptance of those difficult lessons and trials that may yet lay ahead within our development, while also providing the serenity and strength to deal with those obstacles. The concept of reincarnation always encourages productivity and contribution toward universal harmony and order.

The reincarnation process provides for incremental movement away from the negatives of life, constantly building toward life's more positive aspects. It always involves small successive steps, from one finite level to the next, with a goal toward ultimate perfection. This approach does not overwhelm us with the magnitude of our 'total task.' Rather, all the time throughout eternity exists to repeat trials and lessons until corrections and growth are finally achieved. With the perfection of our character as the ultimate goal, it would seem that the quicker obtainment of that goal would be desired, which would also provide accompanying peace and eternal contentment. But such a journey and its timetable are completely left to each individual.

The continual birth, life, death, and rebirth cycle associated with the reincarnation process is either a factual reality or merely erroneous idealistic thinking. Regardless, would it not be better to live life so that it truly mattered, resulting in positive contributions? The potential is within each of us to make a difference and improve the human condition. Attempt to live life at your highest potential, treating others with the respect you also desire, while recognizing that we are all developing at different rates, the basic 'Golden Rule' approach to physical life.

Believing in ourselves, along with the potential of what we can eventually become, can be our greatest asset. It can overcome any adversity encountered, shielding us during misfortune and trying times. Make the best of each day by interacting with your life-path events that are developing as destined, never living in the past or the future, but always experiencing life within the present. No matter how one's life may unfold, remember it is still a beautiful world, occurring and evolving as intended. Be careful and always strive for happiness!

References

Chapter Two

1. Robert Browning, *The Ring and the Book*, Bk. VII, *Pompilia*, line 1154, per *Bartlett's Familiar Quotations*, 16th ed., John Bartlett, Justin Kaplan, Gen. Ed., Little, Brown and Company, Boston, Mass., 1992, p. 467.
2. Philippe Charlier, Oldest medical description of a near death experience, article in the journal *Resuscitation*, pub. by the European Resuscitation Council, September 2014, Vol. 85, Issue 9, p. e155. See also Jonathan O'Callaghan, Oldest near-death experience ever reported is discovered inside an 18th century medical text, UK Daily Mail, July 25, 2014.
3. Ibid.
4. Out-of-Body Experience and Arousal, case-study article in the journal *Neurology*, Pub. by Lippincott Williams & Wilkins, USA and Worldwide, for the American Academy of Neurology, March 6, 2007 issue. Study conducted by research team headed by Dr. Kevin Nelson at the University of Kentucky.
5. Edmund Spenser, *An Hymn in Honor of Beauty*, 1.132, per *The Oxford Dictionary of Quotations*, Third Ed., Oxford University Press, New York, 1980.
6. Horace, *Epistles*, III.xxx.6, per *The Oxford Dictionary of Quotations*, op. cit., p. 261.

Chapter Three

1. Cornelius Loew, *Myth, Sacred History, and Philosophy*, Harcourt, Brace & World, New York, 1967, pp. 32-33.
2. Ibid., pp. 13 & 33.
3. James Churchward, *The Lost Continent of Mu*, Paperback Library, New York, 1968, p. 260.

References

4. W. Raymond Drake, *Gods and Spacemen In The Ancient East*, Signet Books, New York, 1973, p. 1. See also James Churchward, *The Lost Continent of Mu*, op. cit., p. 93.

5. W. Raymond Drake, *Gods and Spacemen in the Ancient East*, op. cit., p. 30. See also W. Y. Evans-Wentz & Lama Kazi Dawa Sandup, *Tibetan Yoga and The Secret Doctrine*, Oxford University Press, New York, 1958.

6. *Papyrus of Anana*, excerpts ref. by James Churchward, *The Lost Continent of Mu*, op. cit., pp. 116-117. See also James Churchward, *The Sacred Symbols of Mu*, Paperback Library, New York, 1968, p. 87.

7. *Papyrus of Ani*, part of the Egyptian *The Book of the Dead*, translated by Sir E. A. Wallis Budge, British Museum, London, 1895, pp. 62 & 64; & footnote #1, Plate 1, Ch.15, pp. 246-247.

8. Sir E. A. Wallis Budge, *Egyptian Magic*, Citadel Press/Carol Publishing, N.Y., 1991, pp. 182-183.

9. James Churchward, *The Lost Continent of Mu*, op. cit., pp. 93-94.

10. Sybil Leek, *Reincarnation: The Second Chance*, Bantam Books, New York, 1975, p. 118.

11. Cornelius Loew, *Myth, Sacred History, and Philosophy*, op. cit., pp. 230, 267 & 272-273.

12. Thomas Bulfinch, *Mythology of Greece and Rome*, Collier Books, New York, 1962, p. 276.

13. Cornelius Loew, *Myth, Sacred History, and Philosophy*, op. cit., p. 208.

14. James Churchward, *The Children of Mu*, Paperback Library, New York, 1968, pp. 210-211.

15. Voltaire, *Philosophical Dictionary*, excerpts quoted by Noel Langley, *Edgar Cayce on Reincarnation*, Ed. by Hugh Lynn Cayce, Paperback Library, New York, 1968, p. 161.

16. Ibid., p. 164.

17. Ibid.

References

18. Noel Langley, *Edgar Cayce on Reincarnation*, Ed. by Hugh Lynn Cayce, op. cit., p. 166.
19. Origen, *Contra Celsum*, excerpts quoted by Noel Langley, *Edgar Cayce on Reincarnation*, Ed. by Hugh Lynn Cayce, op. cit., p. 165.
20. Ibid.
21. Origen, *De Principiis*, excerpts quoted by Noel Langley, *Edgar Cayce on Reincarnation*, Ed. by Hugh Lynn Cayce, op. cit., p. 165.
22. Noel Langley, *Edgar Cayce on Reincarnation*, Ed. by Hugh Lynn Cayce, op. cit., pp. 188-190.
23. Frank Waters, *Book of the Hopi*, Ballantine Books, N.Y., 1976, pp. 202, 222 & 231-235.
24. Sybil Leek, *Reincarnation: The Second Chance*, op. cit., p. 191.
25. Ibid., p. 20.

Chapter Four
1. *The Book of the Dead* (Egyptian), translated by Sir E. A. Wallis Budge, British Museum, London, 1895, Chapter: *Doctrine of Eternal Life*, pp. 62-64.
2. Murry Hope, *The Sirius Connection*, Element Books, Rockport, MA., 1996, p. 213. See also Erich Von Däniken, *The Eyes of the Sphinx*, Berkley Books, New York, 1996, p. 25.
2. H. P. Blavatsky, *Isis Unveiled*, Vol. 1, J. W. Bouton, New York, 1891, p. 12.
3. Ibid.
4. *Papyrus of Anana*, excerpts ref. by James Churchward, *The Lost Continent of Mu*, op. cit., p. 117.
5. Ibid., pp. 116-117.
6. Albert Schweitzer's quote is part of his "Reverence for Life" speech contained in his 1949 book, *Out of My Life and Thought*, per *Bartlett's Familiar Quotations*, 16th ed., John Bartlett, Justin Kaplan, Gen. Ed., op. cit., p. 630.

References

7. David O. Wiebers, M.D., A Physician's View, article in the Humane Society of the United States (HSUS) News, Fall issue 1991, p. 26-27.

Chapter Five

1. F. Max Müller, *Lectures on the Science of Religion*, quoted in H. P. Blavatsky, *The Secret Doctrine*, Theosophical University Press, Pasadena, Calif., 1988, (reprint of original 1888 edition), "Introductory," p. xli.
2. James Churchward, *The Lost Continent of Mu*, op. cit., pp. 113-114.
3. Rudolf Anthes, Mythology in Ancient Egypt, Sect. 4, contained in *Mythologies of the Ancient World*, ed. Samuel Noah Kramer, Anchor Books, New York, 1961, pp. 36-37.
4. Ibid., p. 38.
5. Ibid., Sect. 8, p. 77.
6. Sybil Leek, *Reincarnation: The Second Chance*, op. cit., p. 91.
7. Joseph Campbell, *The Hero's Journey*, a video lecture on mythology, produced by Mythology Ltd., in association with Pantechnicon Productions, Inc., 1987.
8. In Genesis 4:3-5, Cain brought "Fruit of the Garden" as an offering to the Lord, while Abel brought the "Firstling of his flock." The Lord respected Abel's offering, but had "no respect" for Cain's. This act of disrespect caused Cain to later kill Abel, according to Genesis 4:8.

Chapter Six

1 Cornelius Loew, *Myth, Sacred History, and Philosophy*, op. cit., p. 33.
2 Ibid., p. 45.
3 Ibid., p. 42.
4 George Eliot, *Silas Marner*, Ch. 18, per *The Oxford Dictionary of Quotations*, op. cit., p. 201.

References

5   T. S. Eliot, *Four Quartets* (Burnt Norton), per *The Oxford Dictionary of Quotations*, op. cit., p. 202.
6   Socrates' quote cited in Plato's *Apology*, per *The Oxford Dictionary of Quotations*, op. cit., p. 512.
7   T. S. Eliot, *East Coker*, per *The Oxford Dictionary of Quotations*, op. cit., p. 202.

Chapter Seven
1   George Eliot, *Middlemarch*, Ch. 70, per *The Oxford Dictionary of Quotations*, op. cit., p. 201.

Chapter Eight
1   Quoted in a biographical tribute to Mr. Bailey contained in an article appearing in the Lansing State Journal, Lansing, Mich., 1990.
2   T. S. Eliot, *Little Gidding*, per *The Oxford Dictionary of Quotations*, op. cit., p. 203.

Chapter Nine
1   Protagoras' quote contained in Plato's *Theaetetus*, per *The Oxford Dictionary of Quotations*, Third Ed., op. cit., p. 401.
2   George Eliot, *Adam Bede*, Ch. 29, per *The Oxford Dictionary of Quotations*, op. cit., p. 200.

Chapter Ten
1   Karen Peterson, <u>Mom & Dad</u>, Ganette News Service article in the Lansing State Journal, Lansing, Mich., 1991. See also John Bradshaw, *Homecoming: Reclaiming and Championing Your Inner Child*, Bantam Books, New York, 1991.
2   Aristotle, *Nicomachean Ethics*, I.1.1094a, per *The Oxford Dictionary of Quotations*, op. cit., p. 12.

References

Chapter Eleven
1 T. S. Eliot, *Little Gidding*, per *The Oxford Dictionary of Quotations*, Third Ed., op. cit., p. 203.

Chapter Twelve
1 Jim Holt, The Cosmos as a Floating Crap Game, article in the Wall Street Journal, 3-8-1991. See also Jeremy Bernstein, *Quantum Profiles*, Princeton University Press, Princeton, N.J., 1991.
2 Albert Einstein's quote contained in B. Hoffman, *Albert Einstein, Creator and Rebel*, Ch. 10, per *The Oxford Dictionary of Quotations*, Third Ed., op. cit., p. 200.
3 James Glanz, Speed of Light May Not be the Limit, New York Times article in The Ledger, Lakeland, Fla., 5-30-2000. With exposure to a combination of electromagnetic-effects and atomic conditions, Dr. Lijun Wang of the NEC Research Institute in Princeton, New Jersey, claims to have produced light beams that apparently traveled as much as 300 times that of normal light speed through a specially prepared chamber of cesium gas.
4 Bob Davis, A Universal Mystery Is Said to Be Solved, Wall Street Journal, 1991.
5 Ibid.
6 Associated Press article, Universe's Fate Still Up in the Air, Researchers Say, 1994.
7 Ibid.
8 Moshe Hallamish, *An Introduction to the Kabbalah*, trans. by Ruth Bar-Ilan and Ora Wiskind-Elper, State University of New York Press, Albany, N.Y., 1999, p. 152. See also H. P. Blavatsky, *The Secret Doctrine*, op. cit., p. 340.
9 George Hunt Williamson is generally credited with introducing the concept of 'walk-ins.' Initially, the word 'Wanderers' was used to refer to souls of extraterrestrial entities that later reincarnated into earthly human births. Its meaning expanded to 'walk-ins' as a reference to any

soul that might occupy, even temporarily, the vessel (body) of another entity or species. See also George Hunt Williamson, *Other Tongues – Other Flesh*, Amherst Press, Amherst, Wisc., 1953, pp. *vii. Preface*, 205-207, & 210-211.

10 Paul Recer, <u>Satellite finds possible presence of dark matter</u>, Associated Press article in the Lansing State Journal, Lansing Mich., 1-5-1993.

11 John Johnson, Jr., <u>Scientists Discover Dark Matter Proof</u>, Los Angeles Times article printed in the Tampa Tribune, 5-16-07.

12 Paul Recer, <u>Satellite finds possible presence of dark matter</u>, op. cit.

13 Judy Pasternak, <u>New light on black holes</u>, Los Angeles Times article in the Lansing State Journal, Lansing Mich., 10-4-1992.

Bibliography

Select Bibliography

Bartlett's Familiar Quotations, 16th Ed., John Bartlett & Justin Kaplan, gen. eds., Little, Brown and Company, Boston, Mass., 1992.

Bernstein, Jeremy, *Quantum Profiles*, Princeton University Press, Princeton, N.J., 1991.

Blavatsky, H. P., *Isis Unveiled*, Vol. 1, J. W. Bouton, New York, 1891.

----*The Secret Doctrine*, Theosophical University Press, Pasadena, Calif., 1988.

Bradshaw, John, *Homecoming: Reclaiming and Championing Your Inner Child*, Bantam Books, New York, 1991.

Budge, Sir E. A. Wallis, *Egyptian Magic*, Citadel Press/Carol Publishing, New York, 1991.

Bulfinch, Thomas, *Mythology of Greece and Rome*, Collier Books, New York, 1962.

Campbell, Joseph, *The Masks of God: Primitive Mythology*, Viking Press, New York, 1959.

Cerminara, Gina, *The World Within*, Signet Books, New York, 1974.

Churchward, James, *The Lost Continent of Mu*, Paperback Library, New York, 1968.

----*The Children of Mu*, Paperback Library, N.Y., 1968.

----*The Sacred Symbols of Mu*, Paperback Library, New York, 1968.

Drake, W. Raymond, *Gods and Spacemen In The Ancient East*, Signet Books, New York, 1973.

Evans-Wentz, W. Y., & Sandup, Lama Kazi Dawa, *Tibetan Yoga and The Secret Doctrine*, Oxford University Press, New York, 1958.

Bibliography

Golob, Richard, and Brus, Eric, Eds., *The Almanac of Science and Technology*, Harcourt, Brace, Jovanovich, Orlando, Florida, 1990.

Hallamish, Moshe, *An Introduction to the Kabbalah*, trans. by Ruth Bar-Ilan and Ora Wiskind-Elper, State University of New York Press, Albany, N.Y., 1999.
Holy Bible, Cambridge University Press, Great Britain, 1994.
Hope, Murry, *The Sirius Connection*, Element Books, Rockport, MA., 1996.

I. P. Cory, *Ancient Fragments*, trans. by E. Richmond, Hodges, Reeves & Turner, London, 1876.

Langley, Noel, *Edgar Cayce on Reincarnation*, Ed. by Hugh Lynn Cayce, Paperback Library, New York, 1968.
Leek, Sybil, *Reincarnation: The Second Chance*, Bantam Books, New York, 1975.
Linton, Ralph, *The Tree of Culture*, Vintage Books, New York, 1959.
Loew, Cornelius, *Myth, Sacred History, and Philosophy*, Harcourt, Brace & World, N.Y., 1967.

Moody, Raymond A., M.D., *Life After Life*, Guideposts, Carmel, N.Y., 1975.
Mead, G.R.S., *Fragments of a Faith Forgotten*, The Theosophical Pub. Society, London, 1900.
Mythologies of the Ancient World, Ed. by Samuel Noah Kramer, Anchor Books, N.Y., 1961.

Sutphen, Dick, *You Were Born to Be Together*, Pocket Books, New York, 1976.

The Book of the Dead, (Egyptian), also known as *The Book of Going Forth by Day*, trans. by Dr. Raymond O. Faulkner, Chronicle Books, San Francisco, 1998.

Bibliography

The Complete Prophecies of Nostradamus, trans., edited, & interpreted by Henry C. Roberts, Nostradamus Co., Oyster Bay, New York, 1982.

The Oxford Dictionary of Quotations, Third Ed., Oxford University Press, New York, 1980.

The Papyrus of Ani, part of the Egyptian *The Book of the Dead*, translated by Sir E. A. Wallis Budge, British Museum, London, 1895.

Von Däniken, Erich, *The Eyes of the Sphinx*, Berkley Books, New York, 1996.

Waters, Frank, *Book of the Hopi*, Ballantine Books, New York, 1976.

Williamson, George Hunt, *Other Tongues – Other Flesh*, Amherst Press, Amherst, Wisc., 1953.

Printed Articles:

Associated Press article, Universe's Fate Still Up in the Air, Researchers Say, 1994.

Charlier, Philippe, Oldest medical description of a near death experience, article in the journal *Resuscitation*, pub. by the European Resuscitation Council, Vol. 85, Issue 9, September 2014.

Davis, Bob, A Universal Mystery Is Said to Be Solved, Wall Street Journal, 1991.

Driscoll, Paul A., Scientists find first evidence of to quark, Associated Press, 1994.

Glanz, James, Speed of Light May Not be the Limit, New York Times, 2000.

Holt, Jim, The Cosmos as a Floating Crap Game, Wall Street

Bibliography

Journal, 1991.

Johnson, Jr., John, Scientists Discover Dark Matter Proof, Los Angeles Times, 2007.

Lansing State Journal - Feature Article: Liberty Hyde Bailey, Lansing, Mich., 1990.

Nelson, Dr. Kevin, and associates, University of Kentucky, Out-of-Body Experience and Arousal, article in the journal *Neurology*, Pub. by Lippincott Williams & Wilkins, USA and Worldwide, for the American Academy of Neurology, March 6, 2007 issue.

O'Callaghan, Jonathan, Oldest near-death experience ever reported is discovered inside an 18th century medical text, UK Daily Mail, July 25, 2014.

Pasternak, Judy, New light on black holes, Los Angeles Times, 1992.
Peterson, Karen, Mom & Dad, Gannett News Service, 1991.

Recer, Paul, Satellite finds possible presence of dark matter, Associated Press, 1993.

Suplee, Curt, Elusive particle is found, Washington Post, 1995.

Wiebers, M.D., David O., A Physician's View, article in the Humane Society of the United States News, Fall 1991.

Videos & Miscellaneous:

Campbell, Joseph, *The Hero's Journey*, produced by Mythology Ltd., in association with Pantechnicon Productions, Inc., 1987.

INDEX

Author Page

M. Don Schorn

About the Author:

As a graduate mechanical engineer, M. Don Schorn combined his interests in plastics and cars by working for several thermoplastics molding companies supplying component parts to the automotive industry. During that time he continued his professional education with curriculums in Plastics Technology and various managerial programs. Mr. Schorn's extensive manufacturing and design experience led to the development of new processing techniques and numerous patentable innovations during his career.

Utilizing his plastics and manufacturing expertise, Mr. Schorn later joined a Detroit manufacturers' representative firm as a product development specialist. Supplying his engineering input while working with various OEM automotive divisions, he assisted in finalizing product specifications and part designs, ISO quality criterion and certifications, along with direct marketing and sales efforts.

After a successful professional career spanning more than 27 years, he retired early at the beginning of 1995 to pursue a second career in writing. Since then, M. Don Schorn has studied cosmology, paleoanthropology, geology, and archaeology, along with expansive analysis of ancient records and sacred texts. Those studies provided the extensive factual background necessary to write six manuscripts as of this date. Five of those books are non-fiction, including this writing. His other non-fiction works form a continuing series collectively known as the *Journals of the Ancient Ones*, which introduce his unique *Elder Gods* theory, with its fourth volume, *History of the Elder Gods*, recently completed.

Mr. Schorn's only fictional work, *Emerging Dawn*, is a novel of modern exploration, discovery, and ancient revelations connected with the December 21, 2012 Mayan End-Time prophecy.

CPSIA information can be obtained
at www.ICGtesting.com
Printed in the USA
LVOW04s2213301116
515233LV00020B/929/P